the HIGHER LEVEL THINKER

The New View

DOUGLAS REISER

The Higher Level Thinker
The New View

v1.0

Outskirts Press, Inc.
http://www.outskirtspress.com

ISBN: 978-1-4787-1691-4

Library of Congress Control Number: 2013900652

PRINTED IN THE UNITED STATES OF AMERICA

Acknowledgements;

To God who gave me the gift of the mind, the wisdom to listen and absorb life's lessons and now the strength to teach people this gift.

To my mother who has taught me about another powerful gift from God -the heart- and its unlimited resources in pouring love unselfishly to her children.

To my father who has taught me that age has nothing to do with being a man. Honor, integrity and personal responsibility is the foundation to manhood.

To my beautiful wife, soul mate and partner for eternity for her overwhelming support in my quest to change lives and for being my reason to make a difference.

To my sisters for teaching me that even with our differences of opinion, when the wolf is at the door, we stand as one against the wolf.

To my earthly family and those family members who has gone before me for creating the foundation of family pride and challenging me to live up to it.

To my uncle Alois Reiser who gave his life for his country in World War 11.

To Rich Reiser who continues to mentally challenge me to become a better person.

To my editor Denise Rhoades for her effort and success in professionally correcting my untamed writing skills.

To all who will read this book and absorb its meaning and have a better life.

Contents

Introduction: The Higher Level Thinker (The New View)

"Oz never did give nothing to the tin man that he didn't already have."

A HIGHER LEVEL Thinker (HLT) is the ultimate designer of the trickle-down theory, the one who proudly creates responsibility and accepts the mental challenge of responsibility. History shows that the one who possesses this ability, or self-develops this ability, is the one who truly is a leader, the one who survives, and the one who prospers. This is the one who is always reaching for that ultimate goal to produce great happenings and—equally as important—prevent bad happenings from occurring. I will, throughout this book, refer to the person who seeks to enhance and explore this gift from our Creator called the mind, as a HLT.

As a society we have, in my opinion, stopped using one of our Creator's greatest gifts—the mind. In all of its potential glory, the mind has been slowly decaying from generation to generation. That is not genetics; that is laziness.

The mind is one of the most powerful faculties we have and, by my observations, the most wasted. The mind is the most significant factor in controlling life's situations and is positioned at the top of the human body for the simple reason that it starts the "trickle-down effect" of great happenings to your body and soul. A simple change of thought can turn a bad experience into a lesson learned; a powerful ongoing pre-thought process can prevent an accident or a disaster from happening; and a thought of awareness can initiate mending poor relationships or help avoid the tensions that exist in relationships in a family or company. This mental force is powerful, real, and obtainable if you let your mind have a chance to work unselfishly and use this gift in the manner in which our Creator intended it to be used—to sustain life, to grow and to produce happiness for all who enter our world.

The HLT is the most unselfish person on earth due to the fact that they take time out of their lives with a continuous motion of thought every day, to create an environment so that the "trickle-down effect" that they create produces great happenings to everyone around them. By using their mental thought process, they truly do prevent most bad happenings from occurring.

It is not enough to just accept your environment of life; you must create your environment of life. Do your thoughts and actions affect people around you in a great way, or do you, by your lack of thought and actions, create disruption in people's lives and hinder them from reaching their goals and their dreams? I will bet you have participated in the latter at some time. We all have, and shame on us.

I wrote this book in an attempt to not create a new intelligence level, but to make people aware of the gift they already have. We listen to financial experts and we still go bankrupt. We know there are state troopers watching us to maintain safety, and yet we still speed. There are many radio and television talk show experts that devise their shows to give us advice, so that we can find the solutions to the problems in our lives, but we still create problems that are avoidable. To the financial experts, the state troopers, and the self-help teachers, may God bless you all for your efforts. However, what I find interesting are the people I witness on a day-to-day basis and the callers that call in to radio shows. In most cases, they already have the answers they are seeking within them. They just need someone to wake up their own mind or appeal to their logic. Are you telling me that the little voice called the mind isn't prevalent and whispering to you as you decide to pass that car when it is clear that the conditions are less desirable? Or right before you sign on the dotted line for that loan, your little voice of higher intelligence did not question if you really needed that particular item that you were about to go in debt for?

I noticed that people really do not want to leave their mental comfort zone; that is human nature. My question to you is why don't you raise your mental comfort zone to a higher level? Most people would say that they already think at a higher level, however, their actions and their history of misfortunes presents a different case than their false belief. It is almost always obvious to the majority that you are making a mistake, but our self examination leaves a lot to be desired. So the old story of your problems controlling you continues. Thinking is not hard to do; you just need to remember to do it. By understanding and focusing on the next level, we can save lives, we can change our financial situation and we can improve our marriage and the workplace and, yes, we can change this world or at least your world for the better, one mind or life at a time.

The level we are going to explore is where we create an awareness and we can actually solve problems before they happen. A higher level of thinking is all about stimulation and awareness. If you drive a white car, you will notice white cars. If you are planning on buying windows, you will now drive down the street looking at other homeowner's windows. It is absolutely amazing how the mind works once it has been awakened and becomes focused. At a higher level of thinking, you simply are aware of situations. Whether it is people and their needs or solutions to potential problems or understanding dangers and outsmarting them, the power of HLTs is that they use mental tools which we will explore later to mentally stimulate themselves so they are working on the solutions to all potential problems. I did not say problems, I said potential problems. You can recognize a HLT just by a simple awareness in your conversation with them. Where is their focus? Are they dwelling on the problems in their life or does the conversation quickly turn to the search for solutions?

Just as important, do they include you and your opinion in the solution process so that they can explore all avenues of ideas to build a foundation for a well-rounded solution? Once again, the HLT uses a mix of mental tools such as pre-thought, planning, and unselfishness to create an all-win attitude. A positive attitude and spirit is one that creates a safe environment to grow and prosper and a determination to reach all destinations whether it is a driving destination, a business goal, or raising children. Each of these has a goal, a destination, and a final reward. Sometimes the unseen final reward is that nothing bad happened. That is also very powerful and it has no rewards except self peace. No one is mad, no one is sad, and no one gets hurt.

To say, I do not want to go to the next level is to say I do not want to improve my life and those around me. Bold statement? You bet it is. And if you disagree with me, then you most likely are that selfish person and you will always be at that level where life happens to you or worse, you change another life for the worse, and you certainly should not be in a leadership position. Unfortunately, many are. It is time to separate reality from fantasy.

What I see in our society is not just a breakdown in leadership; it is a breakdown in almost every one of us. We are quick to blame leadership or everyone else but our self. The solution is very clear: The top is always where you are. Everything you do or do not do will affect everyone around you. If your actions are of the selfish nature, the effect will be negative, if not devastating, and it will be your fault. If your actions are honorable and filled with unselfish intent, then you will be rewarded with self peace and most likely success, and it will also be because of you. Any road you take will affect everyone around you. That is a lot of responsibility and a responsibility that a HLT takes on every day.

You can stop the trickle-down effect of bad happenings with just a constant thought. I am now in control and I will let my great mind take over my emotions and my spontaneous actions, and I will think about the repercussions of my actions and how they will affect others . If you look internally and search for the reality in your own actions, then that is the first step in achieving the HLT status. Knowing where you are now, mentally-speaking, is the foundation to building the next and higher level of thought process. Whether you are the parent or the child, the driver of a vehicle, a boss or employee, you have to reach for that higher level if you are to prevent misfortunes in your life. The reality is also the fact that you will now be able to solve or prevent most problems. You must at least make the effort to do so.

I will challenge you in every chapter to realize that mentality. I will challenge you and where your mind is now, and I will do my part to create a mindset that will produce great results in your life. If my efforts save one life or one person doesn't go bankrupt or one relationship is healed or you grow internally and realize your self-empowerment because of the gift of thought, I will be considered a success because I made a difference.

I will now challenge myself, everyday to create a mindset that will allow me and those around me to be successful and safe and prosper. That is my calling. I truly hope you choose this path also.

Riddle:

Who is the HLT in this group? A brain surgeon, a teacher or a shoe repairman?

I will get back to you on this one later.

Chapter One: The Reason

"Sometimes you only get one chance."

A FATHER WAKES up to reality on one fall day, when his daughter reminds him that she will be leaving for college soon. His dose of reality begins with a thousand questions. Was I a good example of a compassionate human being? Did I teach my daughter to reason out the good and the bad options before making an important decision? Did I teach and did she witness the fact that I exercised patience before pulling out in traffic and made sure all conditions were safe before passing another car? Did she notice that my attention and priority was always on safety not time? Did I show my daughter what a responsible adult does with money: Saving for the future and concentrating on needs and not wants? Did I open her eyes to the fact that an opposite opinion is another way of looking at the same situation and by looking through opposite or different perspectives, it makes her a more open-minded and intelligent thinking person? I truly hope I gave her the inspiration that there is no ceiling to thoughts and solutions and to not close her mind on just her thoughts only, but to seek the truth, not just her own opinion.

If you love your child, and I know you do, *there* is your reason to go to that higher level as a parent.

A business lady works at her trade with another company. She then decides to go on her own due to being treated with disrespect, even after all she has done for the company. She must go to the next level to make sure that: First, her own company survives; second, that mistakes are not made; and third, that her team of people are treated with respect and are given opportunities—that she never received—to grow and feel self-fulfilled. She also needs to grow and be sharp, so that the company grows and she can pay her employees what they deserve, and that her customers get what they pay for. If you care about your company, your employees, and your customers—and I know you do—then *here* is another reason to go to that higher level.

A man opens his eyes one day and realizes that we have only one life to live on this earth and that his calling and gift is to open the eyes of others to the blessing that our Creator has already given to us—a powerful mind to help create peace, to generate prosperity, and to instill a safe environment.

That man is me, and that is *my* reason to search for and maintain that higher level of thinking; and then to share with others this place that is wonderful and peaceful.

Do you want your child to use common sense when you are not around? Do you want your employees to be happy and prosper? Do you want to make a difference in this world and have self-fulfillment? If your answer is yes to any of these questions, then you have your reason. The way to create a peaceful, prosperous, and secure life is through the unselfishness of a HLT.

The passion they possess internally—which is their need for all to be successful and safe—is why they put out the effort in everything they do, and why they are diligent in the prevention of bad situations to occur in their family, business, and life. HLT is about a constant goal. The reason and the goal need to work together in harmony for success. The formula is the reason, then the goal, then the action, then success.

Let us take driving for an example. Your reason, before you take any trip, should obviously be to reach your destination and to reach it safely. That is the only thought on a HLT's mind and that only. Most people's mind is on what is going to take place once they arrive at a destination, not the journey to the destination. A HLT focuses on every aspect of the journey. The reason, which is to get to your destination safely, must come first. To think too far ahead is where we get distracted. In some areas of your life you must think ahead, but not in driving. There is too much to risk: Your life, for example. This awareness is the force that I talk about that is above the rest. Awareness of the reason is your foundation for reaching the goal.

HLT is all about goals, not intelligence. Goals are extremely powerful. To obtain a great life, you must achieve the thought process of a goal in everything you do. If you do not, you will neglect parts of your life that will affect people and situations in a negative way. I have read how to set goals where you write down your hourly goals, daily goals, weekly goals, and on and on. Those are great and I use them often. However, those are tools for accomplishments. What I am talking about is a mental force where you are living in a constant state of mind of making things better. That is what will change your life and others around you. Every situation in your life is a goal. We create or accept problems in our lives, because we do not keep our mental focus active at all times. We let our guard down with our family, our employees and, yes, with our self. The reason you will want to go and stay in that higher level is because in life, sometimes you only get one chance. Your financial teachers and high-profile business moguls will tell you that most of their greatness came from failures, and

I do believe that is true. Failure catapults you, in many instances, to the top due to the fact that it creates an awareness so that you do not make the same mistakes twice. Finances you can rework, restructure, and sometimes just accept if you choose to live with them. But what about your life? What about the lives of others? The lives of people certainly should serve as a powerful motivator or the reason to think at a higher level. What do you think I mean by life, your actual life where you die? Or did you think I mean your purpose in living? The answer is yes to both. Making a selfish non-thinking move on the highway can cost someone their life, the life of their future children, and destroy the life of their present family—one chance. How about that for a wake-up call? How about that for a reason? Don't you think you can use your mental power to prevent a life from being taken on this earth? There is only one answer to that one, isn't there? Yes, you can. How about saving a life every day? Not saving someone from drowning, but giving your family, friends, bosses, and employees a purpose and a reason to achieve.

Keeping someone from achieving their goals and constantly "putting their fires out" is not much different than causing an accident on the highway, except you are just destroying their life in a slow, deliberate or non-deliberate fashion. If you do not go to the next level, you will not be able to prevent the "trickle down" of bad events in your life. Someone somewhere will do the wrong thing and many people will suffer. It is like a rock thrown into a pond. The impact of the rock causes ripples that grow larger and larger, affecting all around it.

It is the "trickle down of life." Do you want to be the one responsible for these waves of deterioration in your life? If you do not go to the higher level, then life will happen to you and the ones you love. If you go to that next level, you will greatly influence your destiny and the peace of mind and safety of the ones you love. It's your choice, but you need to make it before it is too late.

I often use the word control in this book. However, it is not about the control of others. It is about controlling your life through your thoughts. Self-control is not a bad word, it is a responsible word. Remember, the opposite of control is out of control. For all of you spontaneous junkies, you can be spontaneous and still remain in control. You can go cliff diving at a moment's notice. Just make sure that there is deep enough water down below and no rocks below that.

Your reason to think at a higher level is for your life and the life of the people around you. You have the mental power to make changes, to save lives, to build futures, and to prevent the trickle down of bad happenings. Your reason for thinking at a higher level can be small. It can be as simple as brainstorming to find time for you in a busy schedule or it might be as life-changing as being aware of the dangers on the highway. Thinking should never end and there are no part-time HLTs. That means that every situation in your life requires HLT. Otherwise accidents happen, financial costs are incurred, and personal emotions will be affected. All potential issues or problems, big or small, are part of your life every day, and if either one are neglected, then they can be tragic to you or to others. Solving or, more importantly, over-thinking these everyday issues are not award-winning brainstorming ideas, but they are necessary for a good life. They are proactive and that mindset is what will take control of your life. I have people on a daily basis bring up the simplest problems that are all easy to fix with just a problem list and five minutes of focused, solution based ideas. Your reason to start this mentality is to eliminate the bigger problems from growing out of these small annoyances that occur every day.

Now, why would you want to prevent and analyze small problems? Because it creates a building block of thought so that when big problems have a possibility of arising or do happen, your focus is already intact and activated. In fact your reason for thought is to be prepared for all possible problems or your children and their possible problems and your employees' needs or your bosses wants. I ask that you continue on this journey with me so that you do not have a reason for regret in your life by either an accident or neglect.

I now challenge you to go with me to a higher level and look into your own mirror and wake up your reasons to think at a higher level for your life and others that depend on your judgments and decisions.

Chapter Two: Self-reflections

"The person that you see in the mirror is your judge and jury; and your self-judgment should be harsh."

SELF-REFLECTIONS ARE THE foundation to building this person who thinks at a higher level. To begin this process, you must determine which level you are at now. Are you at the mental level where you really don't care about making this world, or at least your part of the world, a better place? That is a simple question: Yes or no. Or are you at the point where you truly want to make a difference, but just don't put forth the effort? Or do you feel that you are very close to that higher mental level, and you are extremely excited that someone can finally relate?

I would like you to take a mental trip with me and, in this trip, I hope you will begin to feel the transition from self-reflection to self-empowerment and then from there feel what it takes inside to be a HLT. Picture yourself above your home—no roof—looking down at the rooms and the people. Include yourself in the picture, wherever you would naturally be. Look for current problems and any potential problems. Now, make yourself think about and solve the problems or prevent the potential problems you see. These problems include neglect of your home, neglect of your children or spouse, or even neglect of yourself. Focusing from this viewpoint, you will see the needs of everything connected to your life. If you see the needs and you do not fulfill them or if you see a potential problem and you do not prevent it, then you are a LLT. Not recognizing the problem is normal thinking. Searching for the problem is HLT.

I always suggest you begin with yourself and ask yourself these questions: Am I selfish or am I neglecting my responsibilities? I contend we all are a little selfish and we do neglect some responsibilities as a person, a parent, a child, a boss or an employee.

It is now time to call your responsibilities out and make yourself accountable to live up to them.

Now let us visit your workplace with the same viewpoint. Do you see anything you can work on? I bet you see some personal neglect there? Are some people working hard and needing praise or are others not pulling their weight and needing encouragement? Once again, are you doing your job as a boss or employee? We all have to work harder and be more diligent about our responsibilities at work.

It is impossible to see the problems and solutions from your own room or comfort zone. You must go to a higher level. From your new observation point, if a person needs to grow and you do not let them, they will feel neglected and will be forced in a downward motion of no confidence and self-worth. Is this what you want from an employee? On the other hand, if you witness someone not pulling their weight, and you bury your head in the sand, then you have also created a trickle-down effect that will change lives. Even when you think it will help you by avoiding the problem now, it will come back to haunt you at a later date.

In the spirit of looking down at our situation from a different perspective, let us picture ourselves traveling down the highway. You must look at the road and all its activities and that means approaching cross roads, passing cars and stalled roadside vehicles as part of the big picture.

For example, you are looking down and you see a car approaching from the side road and you see your car traveling down the highway. Your thought should be, "I hope that car does not pull out in front of the car on the highway."Because of your view as a HLT, you are now in the position to observe situations better, realize potential danger, and solve potential problems.

Life is simple if you look at it from a higher view. If you are naive and just use normal thinking, you may become the victim of LLTs. HLTs reduce their risk of danger on the road by assuming others are not thinkers.

Now, how about your finances? Are you going to tell me that you cannot list all your assets and debts along with your spending habits on a piece of paper and peer down from above and see the financial problems you are having or see the victories that can occur with the numbers that you are looking at? It was brought to my attention that some people may not know how to do that. My answer was: A HLT will learn; a LLT will not.

I am asking you to look at these issues in your life with a downward view, so you can see the problems and take responsibility for them. Then you can come back down to the earth and go to work. I now, respectfully, ask you take a mental view of your life. Please start with your family and look down. Focus on each individual's needs and wants. Then take some time to determine the best solution to meet those needs. I encourage you to ask others for their opinion, because that brings unity into your world—which is also life changing.

Now, once you focus on one person or one potential problem from your new unselfish viewpoint, your self-empowerment will begin to grow roots. You will grow stronger because you are now determined and committed to making a difference and seeking solutions. From your focus alone you have transformed your mind from acceptance to taking charge. By this simple focusing technique, you will feel more self-confident than ever before and the new you will be born. Your whole demeanor will change, and your mind will stop being the problem and will soon be part of the solution.

You are now controlling life rather than life controlling you. Do not rush this process. I want you to feel what makes a HLT. If you do not feel anything and it does not fill your lungs with air like a powerful song, then your self-reflections are all about you, when actually self-reflections should be all about what you can do for others. That, in turn, builds you up. If this is not where you want to go, then take this book back. The rest of this book will not do you any good, and you will be a LLT forever and for that, I am sorry.

Take this trip now. Remember, focus creates awareness. A person thinks about himself or herself a majority of the time. Who did you think about today? Someone close to you passes away and for a moment you only think about them and their life. Did you think about them when they were living? I got you thinking now, didn't I? Welcome to the land of the HLT.

"You reach up to the heavens for an idea and bring it down to earth and go to work."

1) Self

Begin your self-examination by looking down at yourself, and ask questions that will wake you up, questions that you wonder why others do not ask themselves. Did I lose you on that one? Do you wonder why some people pass judgment on others? Do you do this? If so, are you sure you are not doing the same thing that you are condemning them for? Do you think, now, that since I raised that question you are more aware of your inner being that creates those judgments? Now that you are aware of it, does it not strengthen the core of who you are? Now are you going to stop doing what you judge others for? Ask yourself if you are doing your part in this world. I assure you, if someone knows you, this is the first thing that they will judge you on.

If you are a parent, they will question your parenting. If they know you as a boss, they will question your leadership abilities, and if you are an employee, they will question if you are doing your job. In your self-examination and new viewpoint ask yourself these questions. Be honest, and then go to work to fix your own weaknesses. You may not care what others think, but if you are not in reality about who you think you are, then you will create a trickle down that will not be real and you will get what you deserve. A HLT looks in the mirror everyday and searches for the truth. A HLT asks and honestly answers these questions and many others. HLTs look down at their lives to see where they can improve with each situation and what part they play. They ask questions constantly: Am I a good driver who doesn't take unnecessary chances? Am I a good parent who leads by example? Am I a good child who doesn't take advantage of my parents? Am I a good leader and a good follower? How about simple questions such as, "Do I talk too much or do I not talk enough?" and big questions such as, "Do I create the trickle down that hurts others or do I unselfishly work so that all can win?"

Your self-examination and self honesty is your foundation.

To pretend and lie to yourself is your destruction. As far as individuals go, the truth seems to be in the mind of the beholder, and I am sure that your interpretation of the truth is different than mine. Your idea of right and wrong is also left to your own interpretation. However, I believe that we can build that common ground between us, as long as our truth and our concept of right and wrong stands for unselfishness for all and is not harmful or deteriorates another person's spirit or mind. If those are in your soul—which is what a HLT stands for—then we have the foundation to build common ground.

2) Family

A. Spouse

If you are fortunate to have one, your spouse is certainly a wonderful addition to your foundation to yourself. To nurture your spouse is to build. To neglect your spouse is to destroy.

As a practicing HLT you must take control of your marriage by focusing on your spouse. You know them well enough to know what they want and what they need and if you are not aware of these issues, then you are the problem. However, in realizing that, you have just built a great foundation for yourself.

At times you have heard them, but you did not listen. With your new viewpoint, and no other thoughts but them in your mind, the higher level thoughts will emerge. If you are an unselfish person, then you will begin to see, feel, and experience the greatest feeling, called unity. If you focus on them, you will see their needs and, if not, simply come down to earth and ask the all powerful question of your spouse, "What do you need?" By asking that question, your self-reflections will shine back at you.

For those of you who have lost a spouse to eternity, use their memory and their living thoughts as your springboard to self-empowerment. The memory of others and their wishes and their thoughts is your strength and your foundation.

B. Children

When looking at your children from your new view, you not only need to look down as to where they are now, but you also should reach back into your memory and realize where you were, mentally, when you were their age. Remember the interests you had, the thoughts you had, and the needs you wanted fulfilled. I am not talking about material things. I am talking about your needs for self-worth. Remember how you thought and felt when you were growing up. With your new view, see how you can implement that mentality in your child and their circumstances. By focusing from this view, you will feel yourself become a better and a more observant parent.

Before coming down to earth and taking action, design a plan to guide them—not a plan for telling your child what to do, but for asking them what they should do. Ask them questions and let them answer. You will feel their self-empowerment from within them which, in turn, will not only empower you, but will radiate pride.

Remember, I am not talking about experience, just my viewpoint. Telling your child to do something does not create a thinking mind; thinking does. Too often, from my view, parents will answer the question for the child and will solve the issue for the child instead of guiding them to the most logical solution. If you let them play a bigger role in the reasoning, out of the good and bad situations in their lives, they will feel more self-empowered. Now, what you have raised is a child who will reason out and solve problems that they are confronted with when you are not around.

C. Parents

We spend most of our life being looked after by our parents, even as adults. We are protected against the evils of the world and taught the life lessons and that is the way it should be. With your HLT view, you should, at least, see that and say, "Thank you." That will go a long way. However, now that you are a HLT, you must look more intensely and realize it is time to give back. Just as your parents did when they focused on your needs, it is time to focus on theirs.

Life changes and challenges are different, but your parents are now relying on something that only you can give them: Trust. Be the one that they can count on. Be the one they can confide in. Build your own foundation, and be the one that they do not need to bail out. When you have become strong through your self-empowerment and self-reflections and they no longer have to worry about you, they can actually focus on themselves.

Say to your parents, "I am strong because of you, so now what can I do for you?" In that moment, you have become a HLT. You are now looking at your parents from a different view, not one of nurturing and pampering, but one of respect and simply giving back.

3) Work

A. Boss

Seeing the whole picture is your job. Observing the reality in your company, not the fantasy, should be your goal. Taking a view from above your business is why you are there. This is why you were given that position or chose that position yourself. Now, if you take the time to focus on each and every person and absorb their contributions to your company or see where they are letting down your company, you will begin to feel the self-empowerment and the reason you were put in the position in the first place.

You must focus on each player, if you are going to have a great team. You must also focus on the goal that your company is trying to achieve. Once that has been created, you then can put your team in place using their skills you have analyzed. See what their needs are in order to help them perform the tasks they have been assigned. Keep in mind, each person possesses special abilities, as well as faults (including you). Your job is to appreciate and reward the effort of those who are trying to succeed and to expose, not hide, the ones that are taking their employment for granted.

B. Employee

If you are the employee, you must look from above your boss and look through his or her eyes. We are always quick to judge what we do not know. We presume we know, but we don't. Our superiors usually have a different set of problems that employees do not see. Take the time to put yourself in their shoes. In the search for their mindset, you will raise yourself to a different level and certainly a better or different view. Once you determine what the boss's needs are through his or her eyes, you can go to work on those needs without being told. You have just raised yourself in your eyes and most likely in your boss's eyes. This sounds simple. However, I have seen very few employees look at things from the other side. Instead, they want to continue looking from their vantage point and refuse to go to the next level. The ones that go above and beyond their own thoughts usually get promoted and prosper.

C. Customers

So much of the time in business we concentrate on our own goals, needs, and wants that we lose sight of the only entity that can get us to that successful place where we can give back. We forget about the customer. I will talk about business theory in a later chapter. For now, I am talking about the customer and what they want and need to be successful.

From your new view, look at your clients as people, not numbers. What are their interests? What is their life about? What can you do to help them give back? When you focus on the customer, the rest (business) comes naturally. By discovering their passions and reasons for life, you will create a bond for business that is like no other. As for self-examination, once you care, they will care. Your inner being will become stronger, because it will be expected of you. Word will spread that you care and you have integrity, and this will propel you to the land of the HLT.

4) Finances

We briefly looked at some important and key people in your life. Now, we must look down at some important issues in your life, and finances are certainly one of those. The people we mentioned earlier are all affected by your finances. Although finances are not as important as health and love when it comes to relationships, it can ruin your life if you are reckless. Your finances are the easiest entity in your life to control. It is as plain as it can get in terms of saving, spending, needing, and enjoying. All you have to do is rise above your own wants, look at your finances from above, and simply put it on paper. Your self-examination and self-empowerment will increase, now that you know you have the control to earn more and to spend less. Once you have succeeded, you can feel the power as you purchase an item you have saved for or feel the self-empowerment that brings security and peace. Above all, you will experience the power to give to others.

HLTs will always focus on the big picture and will dwell on security first. They will make sure that whatever their decision is financially-speaking, it does not hurt their family in any worst-case scenario.

Always plan ahead and go forward, but never forget the worst-case scenario. If it is covered, you have killed the looming monster. By looking at your finances from above, you have control of the whole picture. If you do not look at it from this view, you will get lost in your wants, which is human nature.

5) Goals

Goals are something we have forgotten. We get so caught up in our everyday lives that we forget to keep reaching for that brass ring. That brass ring is something we must reach for every day. You must set a goal and try to achieve it or you will mentally wither away. Even if you do not reach it, it is in the act and focus of reaching that creates a higher level mentality.

I had an uncle who was very sick. Even though he was ill, he continued setting up ten-year deals and longer. He has passed on, but his spirit was to reach for success regardless of what most would have said was an inevitable outcome. Well, they were wrong, because the spirit that I witnessed has taken a hold of me and now lives again. So it was not in vain, and he was a success for that reason.

How do you see goals from this view? Most goals are obtainable. All you have to do is look at the total journey from above. If you try to look at your journey from the ground, your head will spin in too many directions. You will get lost in that moment in time and, before you know it, the reality of your dream will be gone.

Lay out your goal, see the time frames, see the hurdles, and solve them before you begin. From this view, your self-empowerment is that you are now in control of your goals.

By focusing on yourself, the people in your life, and your life situations from a higher view, your world and your place in it—along with your responsibilities—should become clear. With this focus, you will create your self-empowerment and positive changes in your life.

To go to another level you must look at your life from a different view. This view should be used in every situation you encounter. Use this view to see your life and your actions, and use your strength and spirit and mind to go to work. That is the life of a HLT.

I hope that I have opened your mind and raised your awareness by showing you a new view, meanwhile stimulating your brain. Now, I will address some realities regarding a few levels of thinking. Let's briefly explore these levels and their characteristics to see where you think you are now.

Remember the question I asked earlier? Who is the HLT in this group? A brain surgeon, a teacher or a shoe repairman? The answer is… I do not know. Does my answer surprise you? The real answer lies in your reality of action, not the false perception of your action.

HLTs think at a higher level in all areas of life, not just in their occupation. HLTs may be represented in all three of these people or none of the above. All of these individuals, if focused, can be great at their jobs. However, if they neglect the rest of their responsibilities in their lives and make poor choices by not thinking, they may never reach HLT status.

Remember, any level that relates to you in some form is not necessarily bad. Usually, however, you will get what you deserve in all three levels. Once again, these mental levels are based on the reality of action, not the fantasy of action. You must be honest about the way you actually think and in which level your thought process actively lives. If you think you are a great communicator, but your family or company seems to drag behind in your achievement process, then you are living in a fantasy world. Until you actually become a great communicator, the fantasy of not being one will be your monster throughout your life. The trickle-down effect will be devastating to your family and business.

The levels I would like to introduce to you for mental purposes are the (LLT) Lower Level Thinker, the (ALT) Average Level Thinker and—our goal—the (HLT) Higher Level Thinker. I will briefly outline the general characteristics of these mental levels, but will only focus on the LLTs and the HLTs as we move on.

"Experience is king. Seek those with it, and listen."

The Lower Level Thinker

The LLT represents a very large percentage of the human race. I am talking about people that actually look and appear to have common sense, but by listening to their words and watching their reckless actions, they reveal their true mental spirit, their mental selfishness, and unthinking carelessness. These people have the general desire to do well in most cases, however, they are lacking in several aspects of their thought process to grow mentally. The biggest culprit in bringing down their mentality is that they are extremely selfish, and all their solutions are directed toward selfish solutions. They do not see that their short-term, selfish thoughts and actions hurt them and others. Their selfish actions will come back to haunt them.

I am going to be tough on these individuals, because they can do something about it, but they choose not to. They allow their minds to get lazy and there lies the true mental tragedy. The characteristics of a LLT are very obvious. They are stuck in the trees with no imagination to see the forest. A LLT believes the world revolves around them. Generally speaking, their goals are not to improve their surroundings—which include people and situations—but to help themselves. A LLT is always blaming others for their failures and always making excuses for their lack of thought. They may be good people, yet they don't take the time to weigh good and bad options. Instead, they dive into most situations with a great attitude and are willing to work hard, but the end result of not working intelligently brings them down.

The most upsetting aspect of these people is that they will dismiss any attempts for constructive criticism. Because of this mentality, they will miss great solutions to issues provided by people who actually care about their well being. This tunnel vision will lead to failure in most aspects of their life. Due to their lack of active thinking, they will be the ones most likely to cause an accident. They will not be prepared when trouble happens and definitely will not take the time to think of ways to prevent bad events from occurring.

An example of a LLT is a community leader who says they will not listen to a person with an opposing view or a politician that only and always votes with his party. This clearly is a weak person who has no self-empowerment and is not a leader. Unfortunately, they have closed off their thought processes and possible solutions by refusing to listen to another opinion.

Another example is the person who would take a chance of passing a car when conditions are less desirable to save a few minutes of travel time. They risk lives and may possibly change a family tree forever.

A LLT is also a person that purchases a large item and puts themselves or their family on the edge of financial ruin, should there be a mishap in their lives. We witness these things happening on a daily basis, and they are all potentially destructive or counterproductive at best.

Additional characteristics of a LLT are that they are extremely negative. These people are in every gathering, every club, and every family. They concentrate on the problem rather than focusing on the solution. They blame others for not having the solution, but will never commit themselves to their own opinion, because they do not have one or they are afraid to take the risk of being wrong.

Another major characteristic of a LLT is they are acceptors. They accept what the situation has given them. They believe they cannot think their way out of a situation or create a new path of thought by asking others. They will, most likely, live with their problems forever and see themselves as victims.

The saddest characteristic of a LLT is that they have a ceiling to their thinking. This truly defines them as a LLT, because they very seldom explore other opinions and seek "outside the box" solutions. Unfortunately, they keep everyone else in their lives under their own ceiling of thought. This will be their ultimate demise for prosperity in their family and company.

If I have been casting a long shadow on what I believe is a very large percentage of this human population that I call LLTs, it is to create a proverbial wake-up call. We are all guilty of visiting the land of the LLT. It is human nature. We are not perfect, and that is also reality. However, I will attempt to strike a nerve and wake up that brain that we all under-utilize.

I do not talk about a fantasy world, because I do not believe in it. I believe that when we make poor, thoughtless decisions, lives are lost, bankruptcies happen, and prosperity is stagnated. That is reality in many lives. It is time someone tells the story of the land of reality and I will take on the responsibility to deliver the message.

The Average Level Thinker

Most educated people would say that they already think at a higher level. The reality is that they would likely only fit in the ALT category. Let me touch on this level of mentality a moment and you be the judge if this is where you fit in.

An ALT is the one who is, by most accounts, a leader in our society and is extremely good at their trade. They will take on most responsibilities that are needed for leadership. When all others stay back, this ALT says, "I will try it"—and most likely will succeed. They will usually solve future problems after a recent problem has occurred. They will make mistakes, like we all do. However, they will make a mental note, so that the mistake will not happen again. They do, for the most part, take care of their businesses and responsibilities. They do have problems, but begin working on the solution as soon as the problem has occurred. Unfortunately, in most cases, an ALT's lack of action causes more problems than their actions. ALT's survive as parents because they preach to their children to be safe. ALTs are confident in their abilities and secure in who they are. They will be thinkers, but fail in the execution, due to their lack of discipline. Their wants may take them out of their rhythm and they may fall short of their goals.

Selfishness and the mighty ego are still very prevalent in the life of an ALT. These are the two reasons that an ALT doesn't stay in the land of the HLT. However, they do visit on occasion.

The ALT has all the potential of a HLT except they still believe their thoughts, and their thoughts only, hold the solutions. Their lack of leadership skills to get people to drop their pride and work together, keeps them from reaching the HLT level. Unfortunately, the small missed-step to the land of the HLT is in not realizing that they can use their wisdom and those around them to solve problems before they happen.

Most likely, they will solve the problem after the fact, but will rarely try to solve the potential problem. They will be the one who will be cautious and aware of the dangers, but will not go to the next level to prevent them. As leaders, they will unfortunately follow the trend of a fellow ALT, or follow their group, political party or stay in their comfort zone, even if they do not fully agree. Generally, their way of thinking will have tunnel vision. Their minds are easily influenced by peer pressure; and, yes, this includes adults.

ALTs will usually have good jobs, a steady stream of income, and will be able to withstand bad financial decisions. However, this will not excuse them for a lack of financial intelligence.

In short, an ALT is, for the most part, where most of us think we are—brilliant on occasion, but too ashamed to say what we did the next. Now, let us kick it into higher gear and visit the land of the HLT, shall we?\

"Great minds have a purpose, others have wishes."

The Higher Level Thinker

An HLT looks in the mirror every morning and realizes personal responsibility. They begin with themselves, but understand that the world does not revolve around them. Every morning, they stand up tall and walk out the door intent on making a meaningful difference in their life and in the lives of anyone who enters their world. They will use all of their God-given mental power to stop the trickle down of bad events from happening in their lives and in the lives of others.

I have faith in you, if you have faith in yourself. I have faith in your ability to go to that higher mental place. I do believe that you and I have faults. We are not perfect and we will make mistakes. However, I believe that we can all go to a higher level and create a better and safer world than we have now. I believe we can solve problems before they happen, and I believe we can build that self-empowerment that creates prosperity in our life and in those people around us.

Let us explore some characteristics of a HLT. HLT's defining trait is that there is no ceiling to their thought process to achieve their goals and dreams as a person. Their goals can be as big or as small as they want them to be.

Is this you? Do you have the desire to ask the questions: How can we make this work? How can we keep everyone self-fulfilled? How can we create a safe environment in which to live? A HLT is the ultimate leader. They are not the kind that we are used to seeing in the movies. They do not stand in front of a thousand people making the charge up a hill, screaming that their way is right and the other thousand people they are about to clash with are all wrong.

All right, that was a little dramatic. However, it seems to be the normal behavior in these times in which we live—choosing sides and verbally fighting to the death. There is no leadership if common ground is not an option.

A HLT understands that if they do their job and create a team, and growth is a common factor, then their job will become better and easier. Then they can focus on another goal, teaching people what they know propels them to then strive for a higher level.

Is this a trait of yours? Do you get everyone in your family or company involved and working on the same team and working for the same goal, no matter what your position or status? If not, why not?

Do you believe because you have the title, you are smarter and have all the right answers? The fact is you do not have all the answers, so seek those who do.

A great word to describe a HLT is focus. They focus on any situation that comes up in their life. Can you solve any problem that comes up that satisfies everyone? Most generally, you can if you focus on every player and their thoughts. What must they have for their internal survival? What will destroy their internal being and—here is the key—what can they settle for and live with? That is the common ground that brings everyone success, not just you. Look at every angle of the problem. Focus on what I call the trickle-down effect. A HLT looks at the trickle-down flow and asks questions: How does my foolish action affect everyone around me? How can my actions raise everyone to a different level? This is not an easy hat to wear, but it is a hat a HLT wears with pride. A HLT will never be satisfied until everyone wins.

The reason HLTs are great leaders is because they are tremendous communicators. They open lines of communication and leave them open—with their family, their co-workers and all who enter their life.

If everyone knows where they now stand, where they are expected to go, what their responsibilities are, and what boundaries they are not to cross, then half the battle is won. Action is the second half. Refreshing, isn't it!

On a personal note, a HLT will always fight, and generally win against the force that creates assumptions. When we assume, we have taken reality out of the picture. We quit seeking the truth. A HLT seeks the truth in every situation. A HLT knows that truth is fact. Until the facts become abundantly clear, then they will refrain from dwelling in the land of assumptions. Assumptions are not the truth. Assumptions may be true, but without knowing it for sure, they are just assumptions.

Case in point: If two experts disagree, wouldn't one have to be wrong? Or is the truth somewhere in the middle? Or is the truth obscured from the minds of both experts? If there is doubt, the truth is shaky at best. A HLT seeks the truth.

Something a HLT fights better than most is pride. You must overcome pride to find the truth and solve problems. If a HLT is a boss, they will drop the pride and seek out their employees' inputs to find the truth. As an employee, they will drop the pride to seek out a co-worker's opinion to find the truth. As a parent, they will include all the family in the decisions to find the truth. A HLT uses a gathering of minds to seek the truth. Unfortunately, this is a rare quality, wouldn't you say?

Financially, income has little bearing on a HLT. It is as simple as living below one's means and being covered in life's worst-case scenario. HLTs will look at ways to improve themselves and create wealth and comfort for their family. They have a driving need to succeed financially in order to help others in their time of need. A HLT realizes that by living below their means, they do not place a burden on others.

Parenting is something a HLT considers one of the most exciting challenges and most rewarding aspects of life. They have one overwhelming defining trait as a HLT parent. They teach their children to be smart, not necessarily safe. Smart takes care of safe, almost every time. They do not tell their children what they should do; they ask them what they would do. That creates and stimulates the seed of thought, not counter reaction against authority. From there, they train the child to use their brain in searching for solutions.

As a boss, they emphasize that there will be no ceiling of thoughts. As an employee, they focus on the company's goal and vision, even though they do not run or own the company. They realize the company's success is their success, and they will go the extra mile to make that happen. The basic principle and honorable trait of a HLT is that negative peer pressure is to be resisted. Wouldn't you want your nation's leaders to vote according to their own conscience and common sense, and not based on peer pressure or persuasive techniques?

As the driver of a vehicle, a HLT controls the road. They will be sharp mentally and look for the mistakes made by other drivers. They will make adjustments to offset LLTs' driving instabilities. (I tried to put that as delicately as I could.)

It is true that while we are on the road there are elements that are out of our control. It is also true that by doing our part we can lower the odds of something bad happening to us. It does not matter where you are in the chain of command in your life—at work, at home, or in a line of cars going down the highway—the beginning of responsibility is with you.

Every HLT must start the trickle down of great events to happen and be the one who prevents bad events from occurring. The characteristic that keeps a HLT on a higher playing field is that they use an enormous amount of brain power to solve problems before they happen. Although it is true that solving a problem is a large part of a higher level of thinking, it is not the highest. The highest is going to a place where, quite frankly, people do not want to go. It is a place where it is magical, but should not be mistaken for fantasy. It is magical, because it is a lot less stressful. A HLT avoids problems by accepting the fact that they may occur. By realizing that possibility, they will be watching for and anticipating the problem before it happens. You may call me paranoid, but to me—whether you drive a car, start a club, run a company, or have a family—every phase of life involves possible problems that will disrupt our goals. Take a moment to reflect on some of your past mistakes. I challenge you to consider how they could have been avoided if pre-thought was prevalent in your decisions.

With that being said, does it not make sense to explore all the possibilities before making a choice? For instance, checking the weather forecast before beginning a trip or asking yourself if you can afford a car payment if you were to lose your job.

Worst-case problems are solved before they arise. These are built in questions that are asked by a HLT. Unfortunately, a HLT very rarely gets his reward, because most believe that it is luck that has determined a lack of problems. The truth is they have fewer problems due to their mental preparedness and pre-thinking abilities.

Solving the problem before it happens will not be seen by most as intelligent, but crazy. A HLT's answer to them is, let us compare notes. Ask a HLT if they have problems. The answer will most likely be, "I am not having problems. I am working on the solutions, and I am now working to solve the next potential problem." This is where I lose most people. They tell me to stop. They do not want to go to the next level; it takes too much effort. That is all right. It is your life, and I will not judge you. However, you will generally receive what you give, and you will most likely get what you did not prevent.

I have given you some mentality levels which we all fit in somewhere. Before we go any further, you must now come to reality about yourself and your mental level or challenge me and dare to tell me that I am wrong.

Tell me that you have never made a bad decision while driving a vehicle while trying to save a few minutes of time. Tell me that bankruptcies are just a state of mind, and they really cannot happen to you. Convince me that everyone in your company or family are all satisfied, growing as individuals, on the same page, and working for the same goal. If that is what you honestly think, then someone needs to look in the mirror, because we should never be good enough or settle for our *now* existence.

Realizing your present level is your foundation to the next.

Chapter Three: The Toolbox

BEFORE WE ENTER the land of reality and strive for that higher level of thinking, we need to instill a few key mental tools. These are necessary for self-mental growth. They are respect, awareness, unselfishness, and focus. The actions that make them all work together in harmony are communication and pre-thought.

Using these tools, you will begin to feel the force that is being created inside you. I use the word force, because it is just that; it is a feeling of empowerment, which is a force. When these mental tools are used, you will begin to feel the change. You will realize where you are now, mentally, and where you have not yet been. You will have to feel the empowerment. You must believe it. These action beliefs are your tools to get to that higher level.

Examine your own inner being. Look into the mirror and absorb each mentality you have been neglecting. Smile as we hit on one you shine at. That is the only way you will grow. You must be honest with yourself and remember your past thoughts and actions, so you can rise to your new higher level of thinking. Do not bury your internal monsters. Bring them to life. Slay them, and never forget what happens when we forget.

"Unlike a river that only flows one way, respect must run both ways or else, like a river, it will dry up."

Respect

You might argue that respect isn't a tool for HLT, however, tools are used for building, and you are building your own character.

When you do not respect others, you open a window to the erosion of your own character. "Do unto others as you would have them do unto you," comes to mind here. So, the question you need to ask yourself is: "Do I want to be respected? Do I want others to listen to my views and opinions?" If someone disagrees with you, does that make them wrong? Respect is listening to other people's opinion.

We have all been in the position where no one listened. How did you feel? Disrespected, maybe? I am not talking about agreeing with someone; that is not about respect. Listening to what others have to say is the garden where respect is grown.

Respecting one's efforts is something our country has deteriorated from in massive quantities. It is true that one has to earn respect. It is also true that we must know how to give respect.

A HLT has the mindset that they will give respect to each person they encounter. It may not even be a person they meet. It might be a person they hear about in a conversation from a third party. Simply give the person that crosses your mind the respect they deserve. Obviously, there will be great disappointments in that quest. However, you have to set a tone for positive outlooks, not a tone of judgmental negatives. If they do not deserve respect in your open mind, then accept it and move on. To degrade them will only show your ugly colors and put you at the same level as the one you are degrading, and that certainly is not where a HLT lives. HLTs respect efforts, ideas, and accomplishments. Small examples are respecting the elderly when they drive slowly, respecting politicians for attempting to make a difference, respecting ones past achievements, and respecting a child's effort at passing a test.

They respect all, with the simple thought process that effort and attitude earns respect. A very important trait and quality that a HLT has is that they understand that they have not worn the same shoes as the one they are judging. If they did wear the same shoes, they may give them more respect than what they were about to give.

Start every thought with one of respect. Look at the positive side of every person, just as you would do if you were hearing their eulogy at their funeral. You would not remember their negatives. You would remember their best assets, wouldn't you? You must dwell on good traits. If not, positive thoughts will fade, negative thoughts will emerge, and the positive will never be restored again.

Awareness

Keep your eyes and mind open at all times for the needs around you. No, not your needs—the needs of everyone around you. Your awareness is the basic principle in creating the trickle down of great happenings. As a HLT, you believe that with the power of awareness, you have created a great place, and great things will happen in that world. One example is in the area of relationships. If your job is to be aware of other's needs, don't you think that it will strengthen your marriage, your friendships, and your family? If your job is to be aware of the needs of your employees or the needs of your boss, don't you think it will strengthen your company? If your job is to be aware of possible dangers or potential problems, and your awareness solved problems before they happened, don't you think there would be fewer problems in your life?

Stop and think of someone close to you. I will bet you can think of at least one need they have.

While you are at it, think about one careless move you have made while driving and make a vow that you will never attempt to sacrifice time for safety again. Through those two simple awareness exercises, self-empowerment should have grown inside of you. It makes your life better when you are aware of the needs of people around you, plus you have just stopped yourself from possibly making a mistake on the highway. That is awareness. If you do this exercise and you are aware of the needs, then you want to become a HLT. If you follow through and fulfill these needs, then you are one.

Unselfishness

Unselfishness is akin to awareness. Awareness is what you need to be a HLT. Unselfishness is the reason for being a HLT. If you rise to a higher level, your thoughts and actions will create a passage for your dreams and the people around you.

To be unselfish in any relationship is gold. It should be your ultimate goal. If both parties are unselfish or HLTs, you will receive what you give. Selfishness should never be let into your home or into your marriage. When you become man and wife, self is no longer. Together is all there is.

A HLT understands that any selfish thought goes against the grain of unity. If, as an employer, you put your selfish needs aside in a company and let your employees shine and grow, you will also grow internally, profitably, and emotionally. If, as an employee, you adopt unselfishness in to your work ethic and go beyond the call of duty for your boss and because it is the right thing to do, not just for monetary reward, then you will grow internally. If both employer and employee are being unselfish and working for each other, then what you have is a strong company. If any part of that dominates the other, it will cause internal destruction in your company. There isn't a more relevant way to describe unselfishness than driving. If unselfishness was a part of every driver, we could save thousands of lives. It is not bad drivers who cause most accidents; it is the selfish drivers or the LLTs. How many accidents are caused by passing? Are your few precious seconds worth a life? We can bring selfishness into any situation in life and it is the root of all evil.

A HLT rises above all selfish thoughts and seeks every person's happiness and safety. He or she may take control of a situation and on the surface appears selfish, but in reality may be doing the best for everyone involved. Seek the unselfish truth in every situation.

Personal bankruptcies are a direct result of selfishness, when your wants exceed the haves in your wallet. How many times do you have to hear the words, "Live below your means" before it actually sinks in? If you did not hear it this time, I would suggest that you probably are of the selfish nature and a LLT. Please stop and self-reflect. How many times have you held your position without looking at the other persons needs? How many times have you failed to address the needs of others and how many close calls have you encountered on the highway because your time was more precious than the car you are passing?

I challenge you to tell me that your life is more important than mine or that your needs are more important than your employees and your wants are more important than your family's needs. Maybe you are thinking that your selfish opinion is more accurate than mine.

Are you now thinking that maybe you have been a little self-centered? If so, let's go to the next level and stop this childlike mentality and make unselfishness a part of your mental makeup. In realizing life is not all about you, you have developed a power and an aura about you that will attract good things, good people, and a good life. If two people are giving to each other every day, all the time, everyone wins. That is a HLT experience. Most successful people and most HLTs believe they were never really happy until they could share their success with others. Taking your unselfish time to think at a higher level, so that the trickle down of bad happenings do not occur to you or everyone involved is powerful. You are at the top of the trickle down of events. Is your unselfish mentality going to create great happenings downward or is your selfish mentality going to create bad happenings? You make that choice. Either way, I know I just struck a nerve. Do you feel the unselfish self-empowerment now?

Focus

Focus is an interesting concept. It is the fourth layer of your HLT. It is the concept that separates the HLTs from the LLTs. We have an idea of what we want, we may even know how to get there, but a lack of focus is what creates failure.

The act of focusing creates a tunnel that leads to our goal. I find very few people with this layer of thinking. The successful all have it when it comes to their trade. They are very focused on what it takes to be at the top of their craft and their job and that is a good start. The HLT focuses, not only on their craft, but on everyday situations. They prioritize their goals and focus on them one at a time. What makes the HLT a cut above the rest is that they spend most of their energy focusing on the solution to the potential problems. They are solving all potential problems before they occur.

Now, if your reaction to this is negative, it likely is because you are letting life happen to you instead of taking control of it. I see the lack of focus in many people who are not successful. It is like a blind person that walks across the room. They will get there, but how beat up will they be when they get there? Like that blind person, if they focus and do their homework on where everything is, they should walk without incident. I used a blind person because their loss of sight raises their focusing abilities. If we focus on our marriage are we not going to have a wonderful marriage? If we focus on our job are we not going to have a great following of workers that are content and fulfilled? If we focus on our driving, don't you think we can save lives? Absolutely! As for my own experience when writing this book, I had to first be aware of the need I was trying to fill. I had to sacrifice my time and effort to reach my goal, I had to focus on what my goals were, and I had to strive for that end result, which is to change lives for the better. I now challenge you to focus on your goals: the needs of your family, your employees' dreams, and by all means…our ultimate goal of being safe. Focusing puts you in that next mental level. It is not a defined act. It is once again an empowerment that you can develop. In each and every task you undertake, focus on the journey and the goal. Focus on the potential problems that can and usually will occur, and focus on the solution to all potential problems and existing problems. With a little pre-thought effort, your life will become easier, safer, and more rewarding for all who are involved.

"Communication is the difference between walking and flying."

Communication

Communication is the single most powerful human action on the planet. I can show you how communication can solve almost every problem in the world today, and I can show you how the lack of communication can destroy nations, marriages, and businesses. That is why it is one of the two action traits that keep a HLT on top. It is an action that keeps the HLT on their own level and separates them from the others. The one that masters this ability will be a true leader. HLTs will set the goals with the help of others, and will let every team player know the goal. They will learn the skills and will teach the skills they learn. They will work on their weaknesses, and will help others work on theirs, so their environment will be strong. They are leaders that share the problems and will ask for help in finding solutions. They will keep everyone informed, so they can all work for the same goal.

Communication is the fuel that keeps the theory of the trickle down of great happenings burning. If you believe that your company is great, then you must radiate greatness downward. The CEO of a company is where it has to start. He or she must communicate the goals and set the vision, and then they must communicate the journey and set the rules along the journey. They must keep in mind that teamwork and unity can only be constructed by using communication. There has to be periodic time frames in place so that people can vent. More importantly, they need time to explore new ideas so that their seeds of thought, mixed with communication, can grow into something magnificent.

If communication is not present, then the monster of assumption will be created and destroy your world. The simple act of asking your employees their opinions will turn the atmosphere of your company from a dictatorship to one of unity. Your marriage is all about communication. You must let each other know what your dreams are and what your problems are. In that act, you will have taken both of you to that higher level. You will then share the same goals or work on each other's goals together.

Communication plays a role in every aspect of life. Wouldn't you like your doctor to communicate with several other doctors about your case? I would. Wouldn't you like someone riding with you in the car to let you know of a potential problem they see and you don't? I would. Almost every problem has a solution. If you do not ask, you will not receive. I now challenge you to tell me communication will not make your life better. Put down the pride and talk about your problems. Work on solutions together—whether financial or relationship-driven. It all starts and stops with communication.

Pre-thought

Pre-thought is the action that weighs good and bad options before any decision is made. This simple act could mean life or death and change your family life forever. Pre-thought could take your company to a different level. Without pre-thought, it could come down like a house of cards. Worried? You should be. How many times have you made a hasty decision while driving or making a purchase, only to say after, "I wish I had not done that." If you had taken a little more time, those pitfalls could have been avoided. Unfortunately, you had that knowledge the whole time. Why did you not use it?

Pre-thought, before any undertaking, is when you make a decision to be safe and brand it into your brain that: "Whatever situation happens, I will always lean to the side of caution." The thing about life is that sometimes you only get one chance.

Pre-thought is where you can introduce the best-case scenario and the worst-case scenario of any endeavor. If you can solve all the worst-case scenarios before they happen, then you have put yourself on the higher level playing field.

A HLT creates a mindset that automatically kicks in when faced with a situation. Financially, a HLT will look at the downfalls of a purchase and consider the worst thing that could happen. They will always move forward while covering the downside of their financial decisions.

While driving, a HLT will not take a chance on passing another car until there is absolutely no chance of known danger. Pre-thought is using your new view and seeing the whole picture before taking on the task.

Before you start the car, make a vow that you will not, under any circumstances, take a risk while driving to your destination. With that vow you may have just saved your life, the life of your passenger, and the life of the other drivers on the road.

Do you go to college for something that will not provide a job when you get your degree or pay enough with the degree to pay off the enormous loan you will have when you graduate? The common sense answer is no, you wouldn't. Well, any clue how many students do and how many parents are paying for that education for nothing? If this common sense action is not taken, then you will create that ugly scenario of the trickle-down syndrome that ruins lives and brings financial nightmares to your family.

On the other side of that, if you use pre-thought before making those decisions or create the thought process that you will proceed with all options covered, then you will start that trickle down of great happenings to your family, friends, and employees. The empowerment will be like nothing you have ever experienced, because by making better choices and sound decisions, you will be in control of your life and be a true leader. Would you want your children to use pre-thought before making life-changing decisions? If so, why don't you?

Now to reach the peak of pre-thought, bring your whole family into the mix. Bring in your employees into the pre-thought arena, and watch the intelligence rise and the excitement begin. Can you imagine the power several people will feel when they are actually anticipating problems and solving them before they happen? By involving others in this HLT process, you have created a team of responsible players that are all working for the same goal and feeling self-worth like you cannot imagine.

Pre-thought takes control of life, which equals success and safety. This formula is only possible if the leaders of a family or company are able to drop pride and selfishness that most LLT leaders possess. They must want to move to the mentality that HLTs possess, which is to let everyone have a voice and express their opinions, so that all possible scenarios are covered. With the help of this unified team and the new vows of commitment, you can orchestrate them all to succeed. This translates into a HLT using pre-thought as a tool for success.

These tools create an empowerment so that when we proceed into the land of reality, we can tackle life situations and guide others to a better life. We must take this empowerment and make it part of us—live and breathe its meaning. If you dismiss any of these tools, then I would say that you are creating disturbances in the lives of the people that you care about, without even knowing it.

If that is what you truly want, then there is no hope for you and you will dwell in the lower mental level for the rest of your existence.

Chapter Four: The Land of Reality

"Reality now is the reality of tomorrow and supersedes all future fantasy."

THE REALITY IS this: I am not a famous personality. I do not have a doctorate in psychology. I am not a financial expert. I am not nor have I ever been perfect and I have made mistakes in my past and most likely I will make mistakes in my future. Now that I have shared some realities of the things I am not, let me give you some of my reality qualifications. I know life; I have seen and felt pain. I have seen the deterioration of friends and families. I have known family members and friends that have died in accidents. I have seen and witnessed people go through a divorce. I have seen successful companies and I have seen many businesses collapse.

My qualifications are called life and the gifted ability from my God to tap into my mind so clearly and reason out situations and to absolutely feel the power of the mind and to use it to serve His wishes.

Now I must step out of my comfort zone and teach what he has taught me. There is no fantasy in the things I have seen, life is real, people cry, people hurt and people die. On the bright and positive side is our future does not need to be dominated by pain, families can survive, most accidents do not have to happen, divorce doesn't have to be the solution and most businesses do not have to fail. I believe naive is the word you are looking for when judging my comments and of course there are always exceptions to the rule; however, I challenge your mind on all of these issues.

I know that even if I am successful in bringing you to a new level and open your eyes, you will still challenge my thoughts. That is because our brains have been trained to accept that the worse will or has to happen, when we should train our brains to accept the fact that we can control and stop the worst from happening. I do realize my task will be difficult. The fact is we all need to have a wake-up call and blast away the walls that keep us from being unselfish and successful in this world. There is nothing I would like better than to say I am wrong about the following statistics. In 2007, 42,708 people died in a traffic related accident. In 2008, 41,059 died. Between the years 1996 and 2006, 1,818 children under the age of sixteen went out to ride their all terrain vehicles and did not return home alive.

Now please tell me and the hundreds of thousands of family members and friends affected by those last statistics that my cause is not worthy of attention. This is a challenge to all minds for the simple reason, the people in these first set of statistics only got one chance, and it could happen to you or a family member today. Statistics show that it quite possibly will. That should wake you up more than a cup of coffee won't it.

There were hundreds of thousands of bankruptcies recorded last year alone. By the time I have written this book in little over eleven months almost nine hundred thousand couples had been granted a divorce. There were millions of people getting sick last year due to not washing their hands. There were thousands of people quitting the jobs they loved due to the fact they could not take the internal battles in their company. These issues are a little easier to swallow only for the fact that the people are still alive. You do get a second chance however on these last references, if you ask the people affected, they would tell you that they were life changing. Do I sound like I have issues? Yes, I do and after hearing those previous wake-up calls, you should too. Have you followed me into reality yet or do you still think life cannot happen to you?

How many major man made catastrophes such as New Orleans are going to happen before we wake up? Man made you ask, people live below sea level and the governing body does not have their main objective as being to secure the levees. Come on now, who isn't living in the real world? Do you really believe that it will not be your daughter that gets hurt in an accident just because it is your daughter? Do you really believe that if you spend more than you make, some magical genie will appear and give you a bundle of cash as one of your wishes? If that is what you truly believe then we have some work to do to get you to the higher level. Knowing that these possibilities do exist creates the mindset for you to use so that they do not happen to you or others. This is not a defensive or negative position. It is an offensive or empowerment position. Knowledge and awareness can be your real world. To argue the fact that life cannot happen to you is where fantasy begins. I have heard this saying come from several parents, "My child knows better," but when I asked the child, they didn't. Real world or fantasy? You make the call and good luck because luck is now what you are relying on. The real world exists in every breath you take. When one person is hurt physically or mentally, that is real. To dismiss it is fantasy, and unless you are very lucky, it will come back to haunt you, that I promise.

A HLT walks, lives, and breathes in the real world. They know their actions can change lives for the good or the bad, and they must take control of every situation that they are in charge of so that the trickle-down effect does not destroy. As we move into the transition chapter, let us visualize from above, but keep our action on the ground and take control of our lives.

Chapter Five: The Transition

"If you do not control the unexpected, the unexpected will control you."

THOSE WHO WALK in the land of reality are the ones who will find peace on earth. They will be the ones that will start the trickle down of great happenings. They can make that happen because they see the pain and do something about it instead of hiding from it. They take on the challenge of potential problems that can affect their family or employees instead of wishing it will go away.

Time does not heal wounds, it covers them up. If you are or want to be a HLT, it is time to wake up that mind and look around at reality. Your spouse is being neglected, your children are not being taught life lessons, your employees are not being trained, and your boss is not getting his money's worth. People are losing their lives in senseless automobile accidents every day and people are going bankrupt at the highest rate in our history. Those are realities, and I challenge you to argue those facts.

If at this time you feel that it is not true, then maybe you are the problem with your life. In life you have to make choices. Now is the time either to rise to the occasion and take reality by the horns or bury your head in the sand, and wait until reality kicks you in the butt. It is your choice to make.

As we make the transition into real world situations and work towards that higher level mentality in the following chapters, you must do two things: First, drop the pride and work with others; and second, stop blaming others. When you take charge of your life, you become strong, you solve problems before they happen, and you start the trickle down of great happenings. That is the only selfish move a HLT has is the one that says, "I will become strong myself, so I can help others."

Statistics say I am right. Everyone knows someone who was in an accident or who made some bad financial choices. Your reaction was probably: "Didn't they know better?" "What were they thinking?" and "Why were they not told?" These are common reactions and statements that you say about other people and their situations, but the fact is, it is probably happening in your own home.

In previous chapters, I attempted to stimulate your brain, to make you aware of your own gift, and to create a reason for using that gift that our Creator gave us. We even created a self toolbox to use to keep your mental thought process sharp and aware at all times.

Now is the time to take our view and our findings, if you will, from above and bring them down to earth to create our wonderful happenings or to stop the bad happenings from occurring. I hope I have raised your thought process or at least awakened it. Now let me give you a feeling of personal control and leadership with a positive trickle-down attitude with that on-going thought process of making a difference and changing your life for the best and for a peaceful existence. We are now in the transition phase. This phase is where we go from the awareness stage to the preventative stage. Here, we go from being selfish and letting life and situations happen to making a difference and taking control of every situation. By that action alone, you will affect everyone in your path of life in a positive way.

I will show you, using real world scenarios, how to prevent bad happenings from occurring before they happen as well as how to make many situations better. The transition stage is where we solve problems before they happen. That is what a HLT does and is: Create the challenge, accept the responsibility of the challenge, and before acting, exhaust every avenue of the downfalls and rewards for each and every ongoing event in your life.

As we enter the real world in the next chapters, keep your thoughts on the preventative aspect of these situations. Keep your thoughts on your ability to make a difference. Do not just read this book, absorb the thought process and create your new view of your life.

Let's go to work.

Chapter Six: Self-leadership

"The world does not revolve around you. However, the world can change because of you."

WE HAVE NOW entered the real world, the world where HLTs live and thrive. Today you seek the truth. Today you teach. Today you respect. Today you listen. Today you communicate. Today you drop the pride. Today you control the road, and today you create greatness downward.

HLTs are self-leaders. They lead most situations to a happy ending, even when no one is watching and no one cares. It is who they are, and it is what they do.

I will now share real-life situations to demonstrate how a HLT creates a circle of energy (not a wall) around them. In this circle good things happen and positive changes are made. This circle of energy can be a distance of a few feet or a million miles away. Whether it is people or situations, you will direct all flows of energy to an unselfish solution. You will create greatness without reward. You will solve problems that may not have happened, and you will walk with pride, because you did it with your wonderful, powerful mind, and spirit. You are now living and serving your

God's will. You have seen your inner self and have chosen to slay the selfish monsters in your own spirit. You are now ready to tap into your mental strength and challenge the negatives in life.

Let me show you how a HLT uses that mental strength to change their life for the better in the real world. As we progress in this book a HLT's self-leadership will be quite evident. The tools we mentioned earlier are like badges of honor. With those tools, HLTs change lives and create happiness and success for all who enter their world. Either long term or just a brief moment in time, self-leadership has many forms. However, the foundation is you and your ability to realize your mental strength to make changes. All good things begin with your mind, spirit, and actions.

"Situations will not be all right until you make them all right."

Let me begin with an example of a major rival of self-leadership called pride. Two men are sitting in a vehicle, about to take a journey to some destination. The driver mentions to the passenger, "I know the route to take. It is the best route to take and it is the route we are going to take." Do you know anyone like this? Unfortunately for the driver, the passenger says, "I am aware of the route you mentioned. However did you know that there is now a detour due to construction and it will take a lot longer if we go that route. Also, did you realize the sun will be in our eyes at this time of day?" The driver is an example of a LLT. Without prethought and without exploring all the options, they have brought pride into the picture.

Pride is like dragging bricks with you on a trip—bricks you will use to build a wall in the road that will keep you from reaching your destination. Pride will raise its ugly head and not allow the driver to admit he was wrong. It is not about being right or wrong, it is about seeking the truth. It is about opening all the awareness of thought with all possible sources to find that solution which is the truth. If only the driver included the passenger's opinion first, he would open up a whole new world of thoughts and solutions.

Self-leadership is based on controlling the atmosphere in searching for the best possible answer using all tools available. It's the awareness that you do not have all the answers. This is what propels you to that higher level, because you seek new avenues of thought. You are now an effective leader and a HLT.

HLTs are not brighter than others, but they are gatherers of minds and thoughts. More importantly, they realize that it takes many other sources other than their own to solve or prevent problems. The greatest gift a HLT possesses is not that they can do everything in every situation. That is not possible. What they do have is the ability to self-examine and self-determine their strengths and their faults. If they are weak in an area of their life they will not pretend they are good at it. They will, however, accept that they are not good at it or that they need work. Believe me, that is not a liability, rather, it is an asset. How many situations have you seen where it is clear that the wrong person is in the wrong position? What usually happens is complete disaster in some cases, no growth in others, and most likely just simple disrespect. Either way, the trickle down of bad happenings to your company or family will be quite evident. Now in our example, if the LLT (driver) takes his pre-chosen route, it certainly will take them longer on the trip due to the detour, which will push them further behind in time, which generally causes more tension, which then trickles down to events that create bad happenings. It is also quite possible that they would improve their odds of being involved in an accident since they would be driving into the sun.

What has happened now is that because the LLT was determined, due to pride, to follow through on his selfish plan. He increased their odds on something bad happening.

If the HLT were driving, he would have opened up the lines of communication before the event. He would have focused on the reason (to arrive safe and on time), and he would have asked for the opinion of his partner, which would have shown respect for his partner. He would have gathered facts and used those to come up with the best possible plan for the best possible solution. Had pride been left out and prosperity and truth emerged into their world, they would have proceeded on their journey outsmarting the dangers that always exist.

Now this example can be used in every situation in life. Please absorb the meaning of this example. I assure you, if you are the one who opens lines of communication, your self-leadership will grow and you will become empowered as well.

The Challenge

Do you exhaust all avenues of thought before taking a trip or does your pride create walls? I wonder how many people who have had accidents are living with regrets due to their pride.

I now challenge you, before taking a trip, open the lines of communication with your traveling companions and check the weather conditions, time the rush hours, make your gas stops before dark, be a HLT, and take charge of your reason.

A HLT's self-leadership has many forms and it defines who you are, even when you are alone. In fact, it means more when no one is there to witness you, because it is now who you are—a HLT.

In this next example, I will drive home my point. A woman driving alone down a two-lane highway sees a line of cars in a tight row approaching from the opposite direction. To the LLT that doesn't trigger any thoughts. To a HLT, it triggers a possible dangerous situation. To a HLT it says that either the lead car is going to slow or the following cars are driving too fast. Either way, the following cars are getting anxious, which usually adds up to a trickle down of bad happenings. In this case, the HLT takes control. She moves over to the right (while not necessarily slowing down) to let the cars following the lead car see her. That is also self-leadership, you look for and are aware of dangers to all, and you take control. You are controlling great events, even if others are not. By taking control of every situation presented to you, you probably omit fifty percent of the bad things that might happen. Yes, it is true. There are bad events in this world that we have no control over. However, life is about odds and I would rather reduce my chance of bad happenings.

In contrast, the LLT would have most likely been anxious and in the passing mode, perhaps causing an accident. The ALT might have been involved in the accident, even though they did not create it. The HLT would have prevented the possible accident from occurring in the first place—no heroics, no awards, just taking control and doing their job.

The Challenge

I now challenge you to rise above where your mind is now and focus on every aspect of driving. Control the road as if it is your fault unless you prevent accidents from occurring. People of all ages and mental levels will drop their focus for just a second and in that second lives will change forever. A HLT will be the self-leader that is more focused and more determined to create a safe environment for all. You will be the one who will make the adjustments to possibly save those who are not thinking. Observe your own abilities so that you are not the one who creates the bad happenings on the road.

"When you accept your own opinion, you quit seeking the truth."

On a grander scale and with many eyes watching, the lack of self-leadership is very evident in the political arena. I understand our forefathers thought process in the Republican/Democrat two-party system, but now don't you think it is a little silly to think that every Republican thinks the same way or that every Democrat thinks the same way? You are going to vote for only your party's way, because it is your party. This way of thinking is the absolute bottom feeders in LLT.

They have no self-leadership abilities. They are governed by the system and influenced by their peers.

Case in point: I watched a Senate committee hearing where the Republicans were on one side and the other half was obviously Democrats. As ridiculous as it was, their seats were positioned as if one side was against the other side, which certainly doesn't bring independent thinking, but only encourages teams. The woman being questioned didn't have a prayer. All she was doing was watching the feud between the two groups. At times she looked like she was watching a tennis match.

I am picking on politicians. However, we do the same thing. We pick a side, usually because of an outside opinion, and not necessarily because of the truth. We assume it is right and convince ourselves that it is right. Then we proceed to attack the opposition. This scenario plays out in almost every conversation. Did you ever realize that the other side has gone through the same thought process as you?

Self-leadership is about finding the truth and not just your truth or your friend's truth. It is easy to join forces with someone who believes the same as you do; however, that doesn't make you right. What happens is that it becomes a one-sided mental feeding frenzy. No other opinion has a chance to be heard, even if there may be some truth to their opinion.

A HLT does not choose sides. They seek the truth. When you seek out others that think the same way as you, you most likely have closed your mind to the truth. Always look at the opposition viewpoint, and then use your own judgment. Most likely, the truth is somewhere in the middle. A HLT Senator would ask questions, listen to the questions of others, analyze their own thoughts, and come up with a conclusion based on all available evidence.

The world of politics is marred by politicians who do not seek the truth. They get caught up in favors and a team mentality. Once they have taken that step, the self-leader has died and most likely will never return. The only way to resurrect the truth and change the system is for our future leaders to stay true to themselves and vote their own conscience and seek the truth. If you focused on each of those senators and their words, you could actually pick out the HLTs from the LLTs. I witnessed only one on each side.

Truth supercedes power or prestige. It does not take political sides. It does not have influential friends or ulterior motives. Truth must reign above all and the one who looks for it is a HLT and has self-leadership.

My father-in-law was a Kansas State Senator and, in my opinion, a self-leader. He passed on before I had the honor of meeting him, so all my respect and knowledge of his spirit comes from people who knew him and worked with him—even those who opposed his ideas. I have spoken with many people who knew him and have read many articles written about him from his party and the opposing party. Respect was quite evident from all of my sources. Even though the opposing party did not always agree with him, (and in some cases even his own party was not happy with him because he did not go along with them), he was still respected because he voted his conscience. I believe most of his peers wished they were as honorable as he was, for he stood up for his quest for the truth. In every case I could find or read about, he fought for the rights of the people and not for the acceptance of his peers. His common sense, honor and people were his partners, not his peers. God bless you, Roy. Rest in peace, for you represented God's people well and I believe you made him smile.

The Challenge

I challenge whoever holds a political office or is in a leadership position to seek the truth in every situation. It is time to change the system and it begins with you, one HLT at a time. Stand your ground. Let the facts and your conscience be your guide to the truth.

People vote for you because they believe you have self-leadership. They hope you have the intelligence to build the house of truth from that foundation.

My next example of self-leadership is of a refreshing young mind without the corruption of peer pressure. It is a representation of a common sense mind at work, before pride and ego are created.

A stormy night in Kansas, tornado warnings probable, a young girl of fourteen was all by herself as she prepared for the worst. She gathered food, water, flashlight and a blanket and cleared out a space in the basement. She turned on the radio and waited for news.

There was no one to brag to, there was no glory or reward for effort. It was just the right thing to do, because it was taking action against the probability of danger. We cannot control everything. However, we can reduce the risk in most everything.

This young lady has the foundation of a HLT. Awareness and fear were partners; the only difference is that a LLT will accept or ignore possible danger signs. The ALT will try to rationalize whether it would happen to them or not, and a HLT will outsmart the probabilities of danger.

Self-leaders understand that the worst could happen. They take action and use common sense. If there is no tornado, you win. If a tornado hits, the odds are you will not get hurt because you took action. Either way you win.

You stop the trickle down of bad happenings. If this girl uses this lesson in all aspects of her life, she will make a difference and have a good life. Although she used HLT in this case, she has stayed in the land of the LLT in many other instances. A lot of that is immaturity and a lack of discipline. What she accomplished was a track record of trust and responsibility in her own eyes and in the eyes of her parents.

The Challenge

I challenge you to tell me that you are tougher than danger, but the reality is that you are not.

I have said these things to challenge you to think about danger and to treat it as such and not close your eyes and throw the dice. You need to cheat danger by creating your own awareness and your own preventions by using your great mind. You sway the odds of survival for yourself and your family to your side, because that is what HLTs do.

"When you bury your head in the sand, doesn't that leave the worst part of you exposed?"

The Higher Level View

Self-leadership is about a HLT using their powerful mind and taking personal charge of the negatives of life. It is about out-smarting the negatives and avoiding them. It is also about simply doing your job against the outside forces, and it is about being true to your own soul and not selling out to the highest bidder. It is about your survival and the survival of others. It is about leading the charge to find the answers and being the first one to drop the pride to create that solution. A HLT has the mindset of self-leadership. It is now time to join forces with another HLT and change your life.

These words cannot change you. You must seek the higher level and the self-leadership on your own and create your own powerful foundation. Lead by example and stand up against the winds of wrong and defy them to blow you down.

Chapter Seven: The HLT on Marriage

"Every need your spouse has must become your need also or else unity will never exist."

IF YOU KEEP your eyes and ears open, life teaches you everything.

If you study people who are married, you can pick out the good marriages from the rocky ones.

Most of the time, you can sense issues in a troubled marriage and can feel the love in the great ones. Listen for the respect they give to each other and the way they talk to each other and you will recognize a HLT or a LLT marriage. It doesn't take long to see if they are on the same page or on two different planets. I have had some great teachers when it comes to the good and the bad, and I have learned from each. When it comes to marriage, I am a HLT. If you do not believe me, ask my wife. Ask her if she feels respected and loved. Ask her how many times a day I tell her I love her. Ask her if she feels she is special and if she believes we are building mountains together! I will bet you everything I own, she will say yes to those questions. If I am right and she does say yes, then that makes me an expert in marriage. I am an expert because I do not talk about it; she feels it.

Remember the first time you met your spouse? Love was fresh and new and you did everything in your power to impress that person and to earn their respect. For a moment in time, you were a HLT without even trying to be. You were unselfish and, by your attempts to impress, you raised your level of thought and focused on the other person's needs during that courting time period.

You raised your awareness and life was good, because you were both doing the same thing—giving. What happened? Did you forget the wonderful unselfish feeling you had when it was new? Did you forget that they were once the center of your universe? Did you forget about the mountains you were going to build together? You did, didn't you? Your mind got lazy and complacent and time turned you from an HLT to a LLT, and it is your fault.

Why don't you put this book down now and go to your new view. Look down at your marriage and remember the time when your present spouse was your past boyfriend or girlfriend. Look down at the time when you were friends and dreamers. I will bet you can even feel the summer air and the instant when you first kissed. Now come down to earth and look into your spouse's eyes and you will see the same eyes you saw back then. At that moment, you will once again have the foundation of a HLT marriage. If you are not willing to do this, then you are not putting out the effort it takes to have a HLT marriage. You will not be alone; I see a lot of selfishness when it comes to marriage.

A HLT's marriage goal is to have a partner who will rise to another level and sustain that level to make their lives full of happiness and prosperity. Your first and only selfish act is to tap into your self-leadership and create a HLT marriage. If both of you are working for the good of the marriage with no selfish thoughts, mountains will be built.

I like to use my quicksand theory. No matter how smart and independent we are, we will need some help in our life. When this happens, it is like being stuck in quicksand. The strength of a HLT marriage is that when one is in the quicksand, the other has a rope and remains on solid ground. You can take turns helping each other out; the trick is to know when to pull and when to be pulled.

This is not just about problems. It is about preventing problems and pulling each other up the mountain to success. The key is to always have your hands on the rope together. The ultimate goal is to be on the same end of the rope to help others. This is the pinnacle of a HLT marriage.

I believe the first step in building a HLT marriage is to examine yourself and for your spouse to do the same. Realize that you are not perfect, and your spouse is not perfect. (Sorry, you are not.) He is not the financial wizard you think he is. He is not the best driver on the road. She is not the best communicator, and she doesn't always think before making a decision (examples only). Knowing that you two are not perfect creates the need for two forces to become one in order to avoid the quicksand of life.

We are going to open the mental toolbox we created earlier to use with you and your spouse. I remind myself on a daily basis to use those tools, so that my brain doesn't go dormant and my good intentions go to sleep and create a trickle down of bad happenings in my marriage. The self-leadership that a HLT possesses has to come from both of you. It needs to be focused on having a great and safe marriage.

We will take the toolbox to your new view using the ladder of communication. Some of you are not communicators and are probably cussing me out at this moment. Others are probably cheering, because you know it is what your marriage is lacking. The biggest hurdle in a marriage is communication. For you to get to that level of HLT, you must get your spouse there as well. Once you are there, you open the box and talk about your weaknesses and your strengths. You create a plan to work on issues that could be causing problems in your marriage.

The second hurdle a marriage will face is pride. You must drop your pride and merge it into the one force of your marriage. Your pride and achievements become one. Together, you solve each other's problems, which creates unity. It creates a foundation which helps solve marriage problem and prevents the monsters at the door from coming into your home.

This is important: You must both go to that higher level together. It is true that each has to do their part. However, if only one goes and the other refuses, then the comments, encouragements, and warnings may be taken in the wrong light and misunderstood. It can create negative issues in your world.

Another important tool is awareness—awareness of your spouse's needs and wants, along with your own dreams and goals. Communicate what would make you both happy. Together, prioritize and work on these goals. Do not neglect potential risks, such as risk and safety. It is easy to say what we want. However, it is what we take for granted that usually derails our goals.

For instance, what happens when you take a trip? Is arriving safely on your needs list? It is on ours. Maybe you were wishing for a new car but forgot about preventing the wreck. I got you on that one, didn't I?

Needs are about goals, as well as material items. If you drop your pride and say "we" rather than "I," your marriage will be changed forever for the good. Be open about any concerns you have, work on them together, and you will build more unity than you have ever experienced. Now you are entering the land of the HLT. However, you are not there until you solve your potential problems. That is when you reach the pinnacle of marriage.

My wife and I get excited whenever we get together, because

we are always working on something: Our marriage issues, our goal issues, safety issues, and financial issues. We create a goal and decide how each of us will do our part for the success of our team. The important factor is that we communicate, even when we are uncomfortable about the topic. We know that if we let the monsters out, but do not feed them they will not destroy our marriage. I do not want to be with anyone else but my wife. We laugh, we cry, we learn, we build, we grow, and we pray together. She is my cheerleader, my confidant, my business partner, and my friend.

"Two brains are better than one. Use both for unity and safety."

Entering the Real World

A husband and wife are driving down the highway when a car approaches from the side road. Are you visualizing this with me from your new view point? The HLT wife (passenger) says to her husband, "Do you see that car?" The HLT husband responds, "Yes" or "No" and "Thank you for the warning."

This is an example of a HLT marriage at its finest. Remember, you backseat critics, the wife has as much to lose as the driver. It is not only her right, but her duty as a HLT to point out potential danger. She is speaking up for herself, her husband, and for the other driver. That is what a HLT does. They prevent a bad happening from occurring by creating awareness.

If the husband's response to the warning is of a macho nature, such as, "I know what I am doing" or "Do not tell me what to do," then he has regressed as a thinker. Everyone who thinks at a higher level should know that two heads working together for the same goal are better than one and, certainly, four eyes are better than two.

In this example, not only did our HLT husband absorb the advice, he responded in a fashion that produces positive energy that will stimulate the awareness factor of the wife. She now will become more alert, because she feels empowered to help them arrive safely to their destination.

I wonder how many tough guys were killed in automobile accidents due to pride taking the wheel. How many innocent passengers have also paid the ultimate price? Argue with that logic, please. Our driver and the passenger are HLTs. They use all of their God-given abilities and the abilities of others to succeed. Are you still with me or are you still thinking about yourself? Your higher level partnership is much stronger than one individual. The goal is not about the dominant male, and it is not about the independent woman. It is about the force that is formed when the two become one HLT unit. Together they have improved their odds of survival and together will lead most situations to a great result, even when others are not putting out the effort.

Sadly, I do not see this unity being utilized very often. There is quite often domination on one side or the other. Usually if one dominates, the other regresses or confrontation happens and the power struggle ensues. Either way, growth goes dormant. Any situation you encounter or decision that needs to be made must be bounced off the other partner's mind. If you do not, you have missed a golden opportunity for success, because the other view point is also one that is concerned about the outcome. A negative or different opinion can mean the success of your decision.

A LLT driver would make a rude, dominating remark to the fact that he is in charge and doesn't need her help. A LLT woman would be too intimidated to say anything. Thus, increasing the odds of having an accident. Under those circumstances, the seed of marriage unity will never be planted. Using another driving analogy: If you have a LLT marriage, you can be in the same car, but actually be traveling separately. In an HLT marriage, you are in the same car, going the same way for the same purpose.

Yes, you could possibly die if you do not seek out the valuable resources that your spouse possesses. Not only that, but without unity, your financial future could be at stake.

For example, the HLT couple can build financial mountains or they can destroy a financial empire. If one spouse has no idea what the other is spending their money on, then financial ruin is just around the corner, because no foundation of unity has been created. I have witnessed this kind of marriage issue on several occasions. Not one of these situations has turned out well; at best there was no financial growth. Their selfishness weakens their financial foundation. Without unity, your foundation will never be strong. We all know people like this; they are our neighbors, friends, and family members.

Once again, I ask you to rise above your normal ground level thinking and ask, "Are your financial goals being met, and are your financial dreams being fulfilled?" You should be able to answer that question from the ground, but you will not be able to see the problem and the answers until you both rise above the situation.

Finances are the easiest problems to correct, in most cases. If you must be reminded to put any financial issue on paper, then you are not thinking at a higher level. The higher level marriage is one that is bonded by an unselfish give-and-take. Until the newest generation came along, most families survived on one income. In most cases, the husband brought home the paycheck and it was important for the wife to preserve what was being brought in. Previous generations marriages had to think at a higher level to survive. This is why I believe our soft brains are not caused by genetics, but by mental laziness. Our wants have outpaced our income and we have quit working as a team. I am not suggesting that women cannot be the bread winner of the family; I am just bringing up the reality of days gone by. That past mentality and the new modern day combined incomes should produce great wealth and security. I will concentrate on financials in a later chapter, but my point is that marriage with true unity will and should produce security and growth. Finances are no exception. With your view and your HLT mentality, together, simply look down at your lifestyle and your incomes, your financial needs, and your financial goals and create the marriage bond that only communication and pre-planning can bring. Do not pick probable situations out of the air. Base it all on facts. Then with your brainstorming efforts, create your path to your goal as a couple. Now it is inevitable that each of you will have to make sacrifices, but that is what marriage is all about.

My wife and I have a financial futures chart that starts with a budget, monthly goal, yearly goal, and a long-range plan. Every month we review how we did and discuss what we need to do to stay on course. If the economy slows, we adjust. If we get a bonus, we adjust. More importantly, we always have a mutual goal. Our needs are always met and, if not, we lower our wants. If there is something we want, we work on it together, even if it is for just one of us. As we are working on our financial goals together, we become as one. Through my observations, I find that in many LLT marriages, the wife doesn't have a clue as to how much money they have or how it is used. I believe the woman does play a part in not knowing. However, it is the man I am targeting, because a macho attitude with finances does not equal financial intelligence. Most LLT men I know are broke, but they still talk a good game without a plan. They continue to dominate the finances even when their ship is sinking. That is not a financial problem, this is a marriage problem.

My wife and I talk about all financial issues. We pick apart the good and the bad options and make a choice together. I consider myself quite resourceful with my financial savvy coming from the roots of common sense. However, I do listen to the opinion of my wife and in many cases, she has directed us to a better solution, and I could not be more pleased.

"Outsmart your mind: Move the clock in your bathroom ten minutes up. Mentally you may be late, but physically you will be early."

On the lighter side of marriage, but equally as important are the smaller incidents that occur every day. If left alone, these can turn into an irritation which leads to other desolations of a great marriage.

Remember, you are always a HLT. This includes even the small items and those small blocks build a wonderful foundation to your marriage.

A good example of a HLT marriage is what I call the Paper Towel Theory. When you use the last paper towel on the roll, do you replace it? Why would I ask such a silly question? Every married couple has experienced this kind of situation. Do you take care of these small issues or do you let your spouse do it? This simple situation will tell you if you are in a HLT marriage. If you leave it up to your spouse, you are not in a HLT marriage. If you are responsible and replace it, then positive growth will happen. You have stopped the trickle down of irresponsibility and have begun to build a foundation of strength and trust a little at a time.

My next question to you is: "Do you thank your spouse for every little thing they do?" Your answer is no, isn't it? Why not ? Do you take it for granted when your wife cooks your meal? Do you take it for granted when your husband mows the lawn? Are you aware that these little everyday gifts build the biggest mountains?

When you show appreciation either by giving or receiving thanks, your days are filled with a powerful feeling of respect. This show of gratitude for each other is what keeps the unappreciative monsters out of your marriage. These monsters can certainly grow from a little annoyance to divorce. That woke you up, didn't it? Good, you needed that.

I am sorry you do not appreciate your wife for the times she did your laundry or when she stayed up all night with your child. I am also sorry that you did not appreciate your husband when he painted the eaves on the house or cleaned out the garage. Your LLT response shows that you believe it is their job and should not be rewarded. Say it out loud and listen to yourself; feel what you just said. I am going to repeat this again: Do you feel what you just said? It sounds a little ungrateful, doesn't it?

A HLT lives with appreciation for all that is done for them, from the little to the big. I may need to work on certain aspects of my life, but I certainly do at all times make an effort in practicing what I teach. I assure you my wife and I are walking examples of respecting what each other does and not taking those gifts for granted. I dare you to test this out: For one day, say "thank you" to each other for everything. If good decisions are the bricks in a marriage, showing appreciation is the mortar. As you begin to thank each other regularly, you will see the mortar fill in the seams of the bricks you have already laid out.

"Call your own home answering machine and leave a message for yourself as a reminder to not forget something. This will help you keep up with your responsibilities at home."

The Challenge

I challenge you to take the self-leadership role and create the atmosphere that builds a great marriage. I challenge you to step out of your own comfort zone and realize that your marriage is too important to you to not take on those inner selfish demons. I now challenge you to go to that new and higher place and open up the toolbox that contains communication, awareness, respect, and appreciation in your marriage. I challenge you to bring up the potential problems in your marriage and work together as one for the solutions. Become that HLT power team that marriage should represent. Your safety and financial future are too important to ignore. I challenge you to tell your spouse "thank you" regularly. I dare you to tell me your response will not be one of absolute joy and self-empowerment. If you do not communicate your appreciation, I truly feel for your wife or husband because you are taking them for granted; that does not build mountains, it digs ditches. I challenge you to crash through the wall of pride between you and your spouse. I challenge you to drop the selfishness that destroys that wonderful feeling of unity that you had when love was new. With that thought, I challenge you to go beyond yourself and look into your spouse's eyes and feel the "as one" you created when you began your life together.

Now you as a HLT power team will challenge old man time and breathe life and excitement back into your marriage, because that is what HLTs do. This does not have to be all about romantic love, but it has to be about teamwork. It has to do with being safe and working on solutions to your potential problems. I challenge you to become a team. Magic only happens when two together are dancing to the same song.

"When turning off the stove before leaving for a trip, say the words out loud, 'I turned off the stove.', This will take care of the sinking feeling you might have if you leave and wonder later, 'Did I or didn't I?'"

The Higher Level View

If you accept my challenge to go to that higher level, I promise it will open up a whole new world and relationship for you and your spouse. The unity you will feel will be so overwhelming and powerful that, as one, you will believe you can build anything and handle everything life has to throw at you. Most importantly, you will control your destiny instead of crying on each other's shoulder. Remember the old saying, "Behind every good man, there is a good woman." I am not buying that. I believe, "Next to every good man stands a great women" and "next to every good woman stands a great man."

My wife knows one of my pet peeves is a woman walking behind a man. I insist that my wife walk beside me. We chose to go through this life together and that is what we intend to do. Stand beside your partner in the clouds and look down at your life and together go down to earth and build your solid foundation and build that mountain back up to the clouds.

Now feel this strength and power in yourself as I review our action theory. Be aware of your partner's resources. Always be unselfishness and continue to give to your partner. Communicate every want, wish or need to your partner. Use pre-thought sessions to consider every pro and con and give your reasons for every situation that arises in your life. Keep each other focused on reaching the goals you both set.

Do not give the monsters waiting at door an opportunity to invade your life. There are the monsters that invade our lives when we do not spend enough time with our spouse or do not live up to our own responsibilities. There are monsters that build walls between us so that communication in the marriage dies. Then, there are the monsters that destroy our physical lives and do evil against us. The HLT marriage does not let monsters in to their home. They use all their tools to prevent the monsters from ever coming in. Please start today. Always communicate, build, and dream as one.

Chapter Eight: The HLT Parent

"Don't tell your children to be safe; teach them to be smart."

I AM GOING to open the doors to the truth and tell you that I am not a parent and due to my age, I will not be. Now, here is where you are welcome to call out my opinion as being the truth or not, due to the fact that I have not felt the emotions of parenthood and have not been through the trials of raising a teenager. Be careful, though, because earlier I mentioned about the new view.

In an ironic sort of way, I can see the forest better than you, since I am not in the trees, since one of the biggest challenges to parenting is the emotional factor when your own child is concerned.

One of the most powerful forces on the planet is the one between a mother and her child. I understand it, because I have had the most wonderful caring mother on the planet. However, this force seems to build a wall between your child and the land of the HLT. You must come to terms with the fact that your child is not perfect, and you as a parent are not perfect.

Parenting, in my opinion, has very little to do with the child and everything to do with you. If you want to see the future of our world, some say look at our children; children are our future. My response is: “Aren’t you forgetting someone?”Saying our future is up to the children is the biggest cop-out I have ever heard. It is not the bloodline that creates the future; it is the teaching from the adults and their examples which produce success. Even though I am not a parent, it is also my responsibility to raise our future generations. I know I will face the criticism, but I will also take on the responsibility of raising today’s children, even though I am not a parent. How about you?

To create a higher thought process: “Do not teach your child to be safe, teach them to be smart.” Smart takes care of safe. This is the difference between a HLT parent, an ALT parent, and a LLT parent.

A LLT parent will assume their children will grow out of their lack of maturity. Unfortunately, with that mindset, they probably will not. The ALT parent will expose their children’s mistakes after the fact. A HLT parent will create a mental process by using mental tools, awareness, unselfishness, focus, communication, and pre-thought and teach their children traits early, so that they will absorb them and become second nature.

I have seen HLT parents in action. They take their child with them when they help others. They teach lessons as they have their child work beside them. They create the thought process that will keep them from experiencing many of the misfortunes that others will. They establish their HLT mindset early with constant communication, so that kind of thinking becomes second nature.

I have always believed that farmers were the backbone of our society. As parents, they start teaching their children at a young age about responsibility. They teach a work ethic and they teach them how to think and solve many issues that a farmer faces on a daily basis. I remember when I was in high school, the most well-rounded individuals and definitely the most stable were those who were raised on a farm. I did not say there would not be issues as they grow; however, the parent child force that you create when they are young will carry you through the interesting years and keep that lifeline intact when the storms have passed.

I can speak on parenting, because I was a child. I was a child that got in trouble on occasion, acted up at times, and sometimes was just bullheaded. Do you know what? I do not remember the times I was disciplined, although I am sure it happened. I just remember the love. There is no greater relationship between a son and his parents as I have with mine. My point is that parents should not be afraid to discipline, since it is where respect grows. I did not say physical discipline, I said discipline. My father spoke of days on the farm when a child would act up. My grandfather would discipline him and minutes after the discipline was over, he put his arm around the child and said that he loved them. My father said that the discipline wasn't much fun, but the love was more powerful and in that system, love and respect was grown.

My father and my grandfather had a wonderful relationship. My father admits the discipline he received was necessary. I find that, today, parents are not strong enough to stand up for what is right, even when it comes to their own child. The repercussions that develop are long lasting and carried down from generation to generation. The parents are to blame and that is where self-leadership as a parent is important. You must decide if you are going to be a HLT parent or not. It will not be easy, but it will be necessary if you want to produce the next HLT adult.

The reason I say that you need self-empowerment first is because your child will test you and try their best to get away with everything they can. That doesn't make them bad, it makes them a child. I tried as a child and did not get away with it. I learned from it. I grew. Now I teach because of it.

Your job as a HLT parent is to hold true to what is right, and that doesn't change because your heart wants to give in. If you give in to their childish ways, you will risk the trickle down of disrespect and bad happenings. If you hold true to what you know is right, then when your child grows up, you will be respected as a great parent. You will have started the trickle down in your family—a tradition of respect and great happenings.

As a HLT parent, you must first lead by example and find ways to teach, not tell. You must be strong, but not too strong to show emotions. You must be honorable and trustworthy and teach your child to be the same. You must listen to them if you expect to be listened to, and you must always seek the truth.

My mother and father taught me so many lessons. The interesting part is that I did not remember some of the earlier lessons until later in my life. That is why the mind is so incredible. You can hear the words as a child and, at the time, not really care or pay attention to them. However, they are stored in your memory and will come out when you least expect it and when you need it the most. You have the best teacher in two shows we all know: The Andy Griffith Show and Bonanza.

These shows taught parents how to stay honorable with their peers and with their family. Even though confrontation existed, Ben Cartwright and Andy Griffith did not waver from doing what was right. They turned problems and challenges into learning opportunities. That is different from today. Parents I witness make excuses for their children. Children should be taught to take misfortunes, mistakes, and unfair people and situations, and turn them into life lessons.

These troubled times are golden opportunities for teaching, not making excuses and condemning others. When someone is rude, remind them that this not the way they should be. If a problem was created due to the lack of communication, remind them of how important communication is in life. If someone makes a selfish move while driving, point out to them what bad trickle-down events could have happen from their actions.

A HLT parent knows that there are no guarantees when it comes to raising children. They are aware that they must do everything in their power to plant the seed of thought, the seed that grows intelligence, not excuses, and that goes for their own excuses for doing their job.

What I can see is that, in many cases, parents are not doing their job. I did not mean that in a condescending way. Spending time with your child and going to the park is wonderful. Watching them score two points in a basketball game is fantastic. Taking them out for pizza is memorable, but it is what an ALT parent does.

My contention is that it is not doing enough. A HLT does more than the obvious. They look for every opportunity to teach and to look for the bright side of even a negative, thus bringing about a lesson learned.

Entering the Real World

As I was washing up after a meal in a restaurant, I noticed a young man approximately five years of age preparing to exit the restroom. I said, “Young man, don’t you think it would be a good idea to wash your hands before you leave? It may keep you from getting sick.” He looked at me with that great innocent smile and said, “Yes sir, I forgot.” He proceeded to wash his hands. A few minutes later when I was waiting on my wife to come out of the restroom, the young man came walking by and I told him that I was proud of him for washing his hands. He lit up like a Christmas tree. When we were walking out of the restaurant, this young man went out of his way to open the door for us and, of course, I thanked him and told him how proud I was of him. Once again, I acknowledged his accomplishments. We both felt good while leaving that restaurant. I made a difference and the young man had learned a lesson. I know for sure that his father did not wash his hands before leaving the facility. The reality is it is that simple to teach. I started that young man on the road to good health. When he was washing up, you could see the pride inside of him come out. I hope that the next time he will not only do it from just force of habit, but because it is the right thing to do. From this, maybe a HLT and future leader is born.

Based on my experience, only one out of every three men wash their hands in a public restroom. That day I made it two out of three.

You are supposed to be smarter than a child, so use your mind and natural ability to create a habit as your tools to get your child in the mindset of doing the right thing. It is your job, if you are a HLT.

The LLT in this example would not care if they or their child washed their hands and spread germs to others. The ALT would probably tell their kids to wash their hands only if they did it themselves. The HLT would always teach their children to wash their hands and then tell them why. The why is what would elevate their young minds.

My second example happened on July 3rd, the year is unimportant, the day is. I witnessed a father popping fire crackers with his son. Normally, it would be a wonderful sight. I often see a father with his son or a mother with her daughter involved in an activity, and on occasion make a remark to the fact that this time together is certainly one of our Lord's most precious moments. Unfortunately, this moment was a disappointment for me because everyone knows that fire crackers are supposed to be popped on the 4th of July. The father had established a mindset in his young son that it is all right to break the rules. Furthermore, what did it say to the child looking out their window at this other child breaking the rules? He very well may think it is all right, too. This is why we are digressing from generation to generation and most will laugh this off as no big deal. I will remind that dad of the no-big-deal when his child evolves into breaking much bigger rules.

This was a day for a father to explain the rules and teach patience, because patience can keep you out of many reckless situations. However, he did not, so another LLT is raised with no values.

Where and when did the no-big-deal develop into the big deal problem? Probably with a firecracker on the 3rd of July, when it entered their subconscious. The father should say out loud, "I gave into my child, because I have no self-empowerment as a parent or person and no inner strength to teach my child to obey the rules." Now, how does that sound with you? A LLT parent would have bent the rules because their mentality is that rules were meant for everyone else but them. The ALT would have waited until the 4th. The HLT would have been the neighbor kid's mom or dad showing and explaining to their child why their neighbors are breaking the rules and how unfair their actions are to others. Are you mad at me yet? Have I offended you yet? Good, you are now thinking. Read on.

My third example of parenting is so very prevalent in the world today. It's about the sporting "supporting parent." Parents today have regressed to the barbarian days. Watching a parent in a sporting atmosphere would make Andy and Ben both jump off a cliff and feel ashamed. I bet you have experienced this mentality. Your son is dribbling the ball down the court in a close basketball game. He stops, shoots, a foul is called in his favor, he makes the free throws and life is good.

Same game, only now your son is guarding the opposing team. The opponent dribbles, he shoots, a foul is called against your son, and you criticize the referee for a bad call. Have you considered your behavior when the foul occurred? Well, I have looked at you and your child has looked at you. When I looked at you, I was not judging you, because I am aware of the passion you feel for your child, but I was extremely disappointed in you, because I thought I was sitting with adult HLT parents. It turns out I was with one-sided selfish parents. I refused to associate with this mentality, so I moved. Now let us talk about how your child saw you. Maybe your child was proud that their parent believes they did no wrong, however this mentality will probably continue even off the court.

Now the question to you as a parent is this, if a foul was committed on your child by another child, did you say to yourself, "I don't believe that the other kid fouled my son on that last play." You didn't, did you? You did not say a word, did you? If you did not, then you have not been seeking the truth. You have made the world revolve around your son, which leads to a very selfish mentality. It is impossible for every close call to go your son or daughter's way. So, you should take the opportunity to teach these life lessons. They will not remember whether the game was won or lost, but they will remember the lesson you taught them from the game.

Do you remember all the games played and lost when you were ten? Of course not. So why would you make a fool out of yourself and bring yourself down to a childish level for something they will not even remember? That is not just a lack of HLT; that is simply a lack of common sense. What has happened is that you have lost your self-empowerment to the truth, gotten caught up in the moment, and that will reflect poorly on your child.

Stand up for the truth and accept responsibility. Teach your child the same qualities, and you will then be a HLT parent.

Now let me touch your heart for a moment. Have we deteriorated so far mentally and spiritually that we cannot just be grateful of the fact that you were able to have children in the first place? Have you thanked our Lord that they can even run up and down the court? Be excited that by your examples, you can create another mind that will create goodness.

A LLT will believe that the world revolves around them and their child. The ALT will only cheer for their own team and get caught up in the moment. The HLT will accept the decision made by the referee. They will watch the game like an adult and will cheer for the achievements made by all the kids on both sides. They will not be drawn in by a "my side is all right" and "your side is all wrong" mentality. The HLT, no matter how the game turns out, will take advantage of the opportunity to teach their child how to be a great winner, as well as a great loser. Effort deserves respect.

The next example is one of safety. Do you assume your teenager knows how to drive on the ice? If your answer is yes, my question to you is, when did they learn that? It wasn't in driver's education. So, when did that lesson actually take place? I will let you ponder that question for a moment. If your answer is no, then how come you have not taken your teenager to a frozen parking lot, set up a cone, and had them practice?

So, are you going to let life and situations happen to your teenager or are you going to teach them to take control of life and situations? If you mention to your child things to be aware of—like people passing when they shouldn't—you can possibly save their life or at least give them self-respect. Well, I was taught by my father and my grandfather about driving, and I remember those lessons today. It would be disrespectful for me to not follow their advice, because it was intended to keep me and others safe.

For example, one summer day I was with my grandfather and we were driving home from the farm on an old country blacktop. He pulled over and insisted that I drive. At the time, I had never been on anything but a country road before. As I continued down the two-lane blacktop, I noticed that we were about to meet an oncoming car. In somewhat of a panicked voice, I asked my grandfather what I should do. He spoke to me in a calm voice and said, "Look straight ahead, focus on the road, and just do your job." Sounds like advice for life in general, not just driving, doesn't it? Well, years later as I was driving somewhere near Albuquerque, New Mexico—it was very late and I had driven a long way—I came upon a situation where I was on a downhill run, between semi-trailer trucks and meeting a semi-trailer truck on a bridge. Almost sounds like a movie, doesn't it? Well, even being older, it still brought up the semi-panic in me. Suddenly, I heard the words of my grandfather whisper to me, "Look straight ahead, focus on the road, and just do your job!" There was, I would guess, about ten years between those two events, but the advice and words were as clear as if they were spoken yesterday. My point is that your child will listen to your words and they will store them and, at sometime in their life. It will come out either in their own teaching or in their remembrance of your wisdom. It is there, stored in their minds for the future.

I mentioned earlier that the time spent with a child is gold. However, it is in the teaching that creates the golden child. I have some neighbors that, by my account are HLT parents. I did not say that they were perfect, and I did not say that their children, who are now adults, were perfect, but the raising of the children that I witnessed was as good as it gets. What I witnessed was a father who not only just spent time with his son, but it was what they did when spending time together. What I have seen them do together was help a neighbor roof his house, and help several neighbors remove snow from their drive, including ours.

In witnessing these giving projects, I saw the father not just telling his son what to do, but telling him why they were doing it. That is called teaching and in this case, it was teaching him how to give. Now the rest of the story and the best part.

Several years after the young son became a man, and while still living with the parents between college and moving out, he was out snow blowing the neighbors' drives, just as his dad had done. I called to thank him, and his response makes me proud just to know the family. He knew what he was supposed to do. A HLT had raised another HLT and this world is now in a better place because of it. Everyone that makes contact with this young man will be moved to become a better person because of knowing him. I believe that with all my soul.

That last example moves me to give you one more example. My cousin and his family were stationed in Germany while in the United States Air Force. He was moved by his higher faith and his higher level duty as a parent. He chose to take his son on a two-hour bus trip sponsored by a church on a NATO base to help build a church parking lot. While he may never be in that part of the world again, I believe he will see the results of their efforts in his own son, because that trip planted a seed of giving into his son's mind. He is a HLT who has helped three entities: his own self-empowerment, his son's lesson of giving, and the recipient of their gift.

A HLT realizes his children are kids, but teaches them to become adults and focuses on that goal. Their teachings of giving and safety will then become second nature and that, in turn, will produce another HLT with the same giving and safety-minded spirit.

The Challenge

I now challenge all parents to self-examine their own strength. Know that you cannot be a great parent until you stay true to what is right. Be a person who leads by example. I challenge you to be the parent who teaches your child to do the right thing, even when it comes to the simplest tasks like washing their hands or putting on a seatbelt, so that it becomes second nature to always do the right thing. I challenge you as a HLT parent to teach your child that rules are to be obeyed and not adjusted for your wants. I challenge you to act like an adult even when passion for your child's sporting event tempts you to trump the truth. If you handle the ups and downs with class, your child will most likely not grow up belittling authority, just because life does not go their way.

Instead, be a HLT adult and teach them about life. Teach them that it isn't always fair. Such teaching will go a lot further in building their character than being spoiled. I challenge you to teach them by using common sense in determining the good and bad options before making a decision. Teach them that they can make better choices for their lives. They must be taught to always do their job so that the trickle-down effect they create is a positive one. I challenge you to teach your child how to give and to share and to realize this world is not just about them, it is about all who enter their world. Giving is a much greater reward than receiving. Accept my challenge and then, by your teaching, you will keep them out of harm's way or at least improve their odds of survival. I challenge you to tell me that children do not die in accidents that could have been avoided. I challenge you to tell me that your teenager using a cell phone while driving is a good thing, and I challenge you to do something about it. No cell phone or no car; let them choose.

The Higher Level View

At one with your wife and at one with your child; it sounds a lot like the word unity to me, how about you? To be a HLT, you must be the one they respect. You must lead by example. Otherwise, your words will have no credibility. If you are married, you must join as one force and be the one force your child will respect. Make decisions together, and tell your child how you came up with your decisions. This will show them that communication is alive and well in your home. Stand tall and stand proud and most importantly, stand for something. Seek the truth, do what is right, help others and teach your children.

You must never let down in your HLT thinking. Focus on your child and create ways to teach them a life lesson every day. Your body can be lazy, but your mind must never stop looking and searching for ways to teach. The effort you put in now will return ten-fold down the road. This is where a HLT excels and where a HLT's mind is focused at all times. If nothing happens to your child, then your teachings may have worked and you will never know. Your reward is that nothing bad happened. Simpler minds think things through after the incident. A HLT prevents it from happening. If your child wrestles with many issues as they grow and are lacking in people skills and problem solving and are prone to accidents, then maybe you have dropped the ball or were a poor example of a parent. All you can do as a parent is your job. You must be diligent in your teachings and trust that what you have taught will stay with them. It is the teaching and example from an adult which produces success.

In every situation, teach them to be aware of their goals before taking on a task. Make sure their actions are not selfish. Get them to focus on their task, communicate their feelings, and listen to other ideas. Get them to consider the positive and negative outcomes of their actions. Your children will adopt these traits and, they themselves, will evolve into HLTs—a blood line created by the brain. As a parent, higher level action can start today. Get your family together, pick an issue or decision and let them give you ideas about the potential problems and benefits.

Direct the conversation to the solution using their opinions. Do not dwell on the problem. With your guidance, they will see how communication can solve almost every problem. Ask them questions and let them answer. You will see how their mind is developing and, with that, you can guide them to a higher level mentality. You will create a thinker and a leader, not a follower. It will be a great time to talk about unselfishness. Suggest an elderly person they can check up on. It will teach them responsibility and giving. Then have some real fun and create the atmosphere of HLT in your family. Consider a potential problem in your life and, together as a family, go to that higher place and solve it before it happens. A positive environment will emerge and your family core will be strengthened. It is that simple, if you want to be a HLT. Do it tonight. It all starts with you.

Chapter Nine: The HLT Adult Child

"Pay back the gift to your parents that you received as a child, and your soul will be at peace."

THERE COMES A time when your parents, aunts, uncles, and friends may depend on you. On that day, the HLT will emerge. You will go above the life of your parents and others and create the awareness that is needed to help them in their golden years. Your new responsibility is to create your own self-empowerment and, with the awareness tool, realize that their time of taking care of you is fading. Your wonderful providers have taken care of your needs without regard to their own. It is now time to give back.

Today, it is time to develop trust. Today, it is time to build that bridge of communication to solve and prevent future problems. Just because you do not have Medicare issues, it is time to find out about Medicare, for them. Even though you do not have a fixed income, it is time to help find ways for them to save.

From your new view and focus tool, consider these issues and make them a part of you. By doing this, you create a parent-child team of unity. Does this sound familiar? To do this, communication and trust are paramount. With these two tools you can go to that higher level and comfortably discuss issues of concern as you solve and prevent financial or safety concerns.

They say that a parent will not listen to anyone that they raised. Well, I respectfully disagree. If you have established yourself in your parents' eyes as one who has proven they are experienced in handling challenges, then I believe you can have mutual respect. Similarly, if you have made extremely poor judgments in your life, then I believe they would not have the same level of respect for you. Therefore, because of your LLT track record, advice from you might not be so easy to receive since respect will not be a common denominator.

I believe the biggest mistake we make as children is to forget our parents are human. Believe me, that is not meant to be condescending. My point is that we have thought of them as being the strongest entity in our lives. We can assume they do not need the same attention as we require—love, respect, help and a friend to talk to. We are so used to receiving from them all of our needs that we forget we need to give back.

As a HLT, you should realize that your parents also want to feel important and respected. They should feel loved and appreciated. They should be told that they can trust and confide in you. Reassure them of that and never betray that trust.

The transition from them giving to receiving is a wonderful thing. It should be as welcome as the circle of life. The process starts with them providing all your needs, then the awkward years of you thinking you know everything that you really do not. Then, as they release a little responsibility as you prove yourself more independent, something beautiful happens. The parents' teachings become fewer, the ruffled feathers of the teenage years smooth out, and respectable friends emerge. What you both seek as HLTs is respect. You will respect their years of wisdom and experience, and they will respect that you are now an adult. Once the respect is mutual, a whole new world is created. This is where the HLT in you shines. This is where the HLT in you uses communication to transpose their wants and needs into your wants and needs. Absorb their point-of-view and help them solve situations from there.

If you can build this power team, your bond as parent and child will grow strong. There will be a balancing act between their ideas and yours, but as a self-leader, look at both sides and opinions to decide what will bring about success. If you have earned their trust and sincerity, then your team will be strong to face future challenges.

As we enter the HLT adult child's world, we will look through our parents' eyes and do everything in our power to: "Not make Mama (or Papa) cry." This is why a HLT plays guardian angel and makes sure concerns are being addressed. Along with taking care of your own life issues, you take on the concerns of your parents.

Of course, parents do not always need constant attention. The important lesson is that adult children need to be aware of their responsibility to care for their elderly parents. The circle of life means that as a parent you raise your children, but you also need to be a responsible child. To do this, you may have to wear both hats at one time. A HLT will do both with the intention of stopping the trickle down of bad happenings to your child and your parents.

Entering the Real World

Today, many elderly adults are being scammed out of their lifetime savings. What about your parents? Made you think, didn't I? Out of the thousands that got scammed, I wonder how many had adult children who didn't know about it until it was too late. How many of these incidents could have been prevented if their child had looked above their parents' home and realized the dangers that lurk in every phone call or letter sent to their parents? Yes, it is your fault. You are the one that should have taken the effort to make your parents aware of the dangers. We all will lose a little of our common sense practices when the circle of life comes around. Big hearts, compassion, and loneliness may make us susceptible to fraud. As an adult child, you have the responsibility to take charge. Your job is to become educated in such matters that can affect your parents. Your HLT job is to create awareness and plant a seed of thought for your parents in terms of danger. This is not a fun place to be. At one time, your parents told you to be careful and guided you through life's dangers. Now they need your friendship and your guidance. As a HLT, step up and take charge without taking over.

Communication is key. Tap into your mental sources and become the leader that your parents raised you to be. Create an environment with your parents that is one of unity. Tell them your concerns, tell them of your love for them, and ask them to work with you to create a safe environment for them. This is not only for them, but for your mental well being. Getting scammed or being taken advantage of is quite common among the elderly. It happens very quickly. Awareness could prevent such financial tragedies. You do not need to know everything they own. However, it is good to have some information to be helpful.

I am not suggesting you take over. It is a partnership created between both parties, so that they can live in a world where respect and caution rule. A LLT would assume that everything is okay and continue on their selfish path, not worrying about their parents' issues. The ALT will add their opinion when it comes up in conversation and, most likely, will let the issue die and hope for the best. The HLT will take charge of the situation without taking charge of their parents and while respecting their opinions. They will seek out other professional opinions and respectfully ask to be at meetings with representatives in order to ask more questions.

I am not just talking about scams. Familiarize yourself with Medicare issues, the medicines your parents take, and their overall health information. This is not so you can tell them what to do, but so you can learn and be helpful. They gave their time and effort for you, so it is now time to give yours.

Is your parent being scammed right now? Odds say they are. In your quest to be that HLT adult child, there are many life issues that concern your parents. The trickle down of bad happenings seems to happen faster with the elderly with more devastating results.

The trickle down began for elderly friends of mine when the wife fell and hurt her hip. She spent time in the hospital and in rehabilitation before returning home. I would like to think that a HLT intervention by the children would have prevented the next two falls, which led to two very long hospital stays and then into assisted living. The trickle down that followed was due to a lack of awareness of safety. Both falls that started this downward spiral could have been prevented if the adult children would have created the "what ifs" for their parents. If awareness was initiated, a plan of safety could have been created. It is quite possible that these two wonderful people could have retained their freedom and remained living at home.

We must work together as a team (parent and child) to become a HLT force. In this example, the LLT lets life happen to their parents. They continue to live in a fantasy world where their parents are not getting older and do not require support. Of course, when reality hits, it will be a tough pill to swallow.

The ALT would give their parents their complete attention after something happened. They would feel bad and wish they had done something to prevent the accident. The HLT will imagine the worst-case scenarios and work to solve them before disaster strikes. They will seek out potential problems and make their parents aware of them. By doing this they can feel confident that they have done their part in being a great adult child and a HLT.

At least, do not bring your parents into your world of selfish wants and bad choices. For example, do not ask your parents to co-sign a financial loan for you. Remember, this is your want, not the want of your parents. So, be a HLT and stand up on your own two feet. Do not cause them stress by your wants. If you play on their heart strings and financial strings, your relationship will be destroyed, not to mention your self-respect.

HLTs will not place financial burdens on others, especially their parents. Your gift to your parents is to be responsible and strong for them. Putting yourself in a poor financial position due to your LLT and then transferring that financial irresponsibility to your parents puts you at the bottom of the thinkers.

Your parents have worked their whole lives to create a good life for you and then to find financial peace for themselves. They do not need to risk their financial future for you. I see parents making bad financial choices for the sake of their children, and that is wrong.

The LLT will make the parent feel guilty if they do not help with their debts or babysit. They develop a pattern of dependency and, once that cat is out of the bag, you will not get it back in. The trickle-down pattern is an ugly one where the adult child never grows up.

The HLT will live in such a way that they do not put others in an awkward position. A HLT will keep their wants low and cover their back if things would go wrong. They understand they have to live with their choices. Others should not have to pay for their mistakes. This helps them make better choices, which strengthens their own foundation.

The higher place I talk about is where parents can help, but are not forced to help for the wrong reasons. The HLT will do everything in their power to find their own solutions, but if assistance is needed, they will be overwhelmed with respect for their parents and do everything to pay back the debt. Taking them for granted would not enter their mind.

Some situations turn our world upside down: health issues, getting laid off from work, etc.—circumstances over which you have no control. These things happen. Instead, I am talking about the selfish wants and difficulties in families. If you are sick and cannot work, people will answer the call, but if you buy a car and cannot afford it, that decision is self-inflicted. That burden should not be put on your parents. If a HLT buys a car they cannot afford, they will sell the car once they realize their mistake. That is what a HLT adult child does.

The HLT Teenager

On a rainy night, a young man and his friend jumped into the backseat of a hopped up car owned by another friend. After a short while, it became quite evident that the driver had too much excitement built up inside, whether natural or not. So even in a driving rainstorm, the two young men in the backseat decided that the situation, which seemed innocent at the time, had bad trickle-down vibes to it. After a brief conversation and mental collaboration, the two insisted that their friend pull over and let them out of the car. Mind you, the self-empowerment was more overwhelming than the conditions. The two got out, got soaked, and went home. Later that evening, they received a call that their friends had headed down a busy road at a great speed, lost control, and hit a tree. They survived, but not without long-term injuries. The next day, the two who got out of the vehicle were checking out the damage to the car. What they experienced was life changing. I am not just talking about the destruction of a very beautiful car; it was the realization that there was now no back seat to the car. The place they had been sitting in was gone.

Please take a moment to think about that: No back seat. I will bet my mother will cry when she reads this. Yes, one of those young men was me. I hope my mother cries for two reasons: The first, because of joy that I did not die, and the second, because of pride that I made the HLT choice that evening. The moment when I saw the car is when I realized I could control my life or else life would have happened to me. Because of the teachings of my parents and because we reasoned out the situation and weighed the risks, we were able to move on in our life. Can you imagine the trickle-down effect if we had made the wrong choice that night. Yes, I would have made my mama cry.

I do not blame those friends that I was with that night. They made their choice; we made ours. We can lead by example, and I only hope that they also learned a lesson that night. The peer pressure was intense that evening, but a HLT only listens to common sense. Only thirty years later have I realized my calling to open minds and, hopefully. Prevent tragedies from occurring. If I can realize that at an early age, I hold out hope for the young adults of this world for a bright tomorrow.

I am not living in a fantasy world when I say there is an abundance of teenage HLT's, in this world, in fact I believe that we need to create the future HLTs. I hope I am wrong when I say that most adults probably are too perfect to change. I talk about the team that HLTs can create. This team is a give-and-take between teenagers and their parents, and it is also one of trust.

As a young adult, you can create a family team by doing your part. Young adults seem to leave most situations up to the parents. However, adults have just as many problems as teenagers. Remember the top is always where you are, that being said, it is not your responsibility to tell the adult what to do. It is your responsibility to do the right thing. You need to take control of your destiny. You become the leader even if it goes against your peers. You create a family team to help you and your parents through these interesting years.

As a young adult, you must also understand reality. Your mind is inexperienced, not ignorant. You must tap into and learn from the minds of those adults that have experienced what you are or will be going through. Take words of wisdom from others and analyze them for yourself, but by all means use it. Become stronger by their past mistakes and avoid them. As a HLT, don't you think that someone who loves you and takes time out of their life to give you advice would only want the best for you? Do you not think that if you had a child you would not want them to be safe and prosper?

Remember, HLTs look at both sides of an issue. If you are a HLT, you will create an environment in which you can work with your parents to make both parties feel comfortable. Together, decide on a curfew. Work with them to create the bond that will be held together by a wonderful action called trust. As a HLT you will do what you say because it is the character of a HLT to back up their words with action. Once trust is created, you will get more freedoms and you can build a powerful relationship from there. Betray the trust and you will be reduced back to a child and will have to start all over again. It is very empowering to become the leader of good. It will be a high that no drugs or alcohol can produce. The friends that become your friends in this environment will be ones you can trust. No other environment can be trusted. Good is not about money or your parents' status in the community. It is about what is right, and that comes from your conscience and your soul.

I have done things or said things and judged things in my life that will haunt me forever. I should have stood up for the weak, even against the ones I thought were my friends at the time. I did not, but that will never happen again. I will challenge my friends if they are selfish, judgmental, careless, or prejudiced, because they are wrong. You will not be popular, but stand up with your head held high and say, "I stand for good" and tell them why.

The one thing that must be avoided if you are to become a HLT is to think you are not the decision maker in your world. That kind of thinking causes you to deny your responsibility in this world. Instead, take care of your responsibilities, and you will have a better life. Do not ask for money or trust, earn them.

The Challenge

I challenge everyone: Do not make your mama cry. I challenge you to make your parents proud. I challenge you to start giving back to them because they gave to you. I challenge you to rise above your own needs and rise above their life and search for their needs as well as some of their wants. I challenge you to be their best friend and to never betray their trust. I challenge your own self-empowerment to take charge of building that team through communication to create a safe environment. I challenge you to help them in all aspects of their life which includes exploring options to solve their financial situation. I challenge you to maintain your life and discipline in the way that reduces the odds that your parents will need to help fix your bad choices. Be as safe as possible. Do not cause them pain and sorrow. An HLT thinks about those who care for them and in this chapter, especially when those people are their parents.

The Higher Level View

It is time to stand up and take charge as a HLT. Think ahead. Deal with your parents issues as if they were your own.

They lived their whole life making sure your needs were fulfilled and that you were happy. It is time to help them achieve their dreams. Most great parents will say, "I just want my kids to be ok." Well then HLT, start living like a HLT and fulfill their dreams. Your parents want the best for you whether they are still on this earth or home with their Lord. It is your job to take care of that wish and make their spirit proud. By all means, "Do not make your mama cry."

Chapter Ten: The HLT Elder

ONCE AGAIN, I am sure that I will face criticism with my elderly readers since I am only middle aged. However, I have seen from my higher view that my opinions have merit. Even though you have enormous knowledge and experience, my hope is that you will listen to another opinion to make your life safer and more self fulfilled. I have always had respect for my elders. I can honestly say that over three-fourths of my closest friends are elderly. Unfortunately, I feel the pain and the negative spirits that go along with being elderly, not to mention the accidents that could have been prevented.

The reason I am writing this chapter is because I care about each and every one of you. If I can prevent one accident or one ounce of pain then my efforts will be rewarded.

The circle of life is not an easy pill to swallow. However, it will not change. I believe you can walk the walk and talk the talk of a HLT if you come to terms with the reality of your physical limitations. These physical limitations can certainly be a negative. However, I believe we can take that realization and combine that with your own past experiences. Realization and limitation is important to your self-empowerment and can be life changing for the good.

This chapter has nothing to do with lack of intelligence, ability or common sense. As we age we will get slower and, by nature, become less focused. Pride and stubbornness may still be culprits that create problems in our life. These will be magnified as we grow older. We live our lives by our own rules and that will never change. The problem is instead of changing our own rules to fit our life, we hold on to the past and this separates the LLTs from the HLTs. It is time to set the example that you have set all of your life for your children and grandchildren. Together build a strong foundation by using your reality and create your self-empowerment as a HLT.

Limitations and Realizations

Limitations

"Understanding your limitations is your foundation; realizing your potential is your strength."

The first thing I need to do is scare the heck out of you. I heard it is called tough love and I believe in it. In order to reach any positive mode in your life you must cover the negatives and accept and be aware of all the dangers. Once the dangers are identified and taken care of, then solutions and preventive measures can be developed and activated and a more peaceful and safe existence can begin.

I know I walk a fine line here between limitations and no limitations. The difference will become clear and very empowering as you read on. The limitations I talk about can produce the trickle down of bad happenings. Your awareness tool must be carried with you at all times and should never be put back in the toolbox.

As you get older, the odds increase that the simplest tasks that were taken for granted in the earlier years can be catastrophic to your well being. You must go to that higher level before it is too late. I am trying to scare you while, at the same time, explaining to you that if you create your toolbox and build your empowerment you will now control all the entities that can harm you. Your mental toughness that you already possess will get you through the trying years and put a shine on the gold in your older years. You will realize that the mental toughness that you possess will supersede the physical challenges that life will throw at you.

Do not attack me. You know it is true. The elderly get caught in the trap, because they do not drop their pride and create the reality that we cannot still do the things we used to do. Obviously there are exceptions, but eventually you will enter into the circle of life. It is now time to take charge of life instead of living in fear of life happening to you. I have seen the most intelligent people I have ever met get sucked into this transition phase without knowing it and disaster happened. It happens gradually and then it may be too late.

A HLT accepts the inevitable and prepares their life for what is to come. They take the self-leadership role and in the awareness of life is their empowerment. Seek out and destroy the monsters that pride and stubbornness will allow into your life and do it now. I want you to understand that I had to speak of the dangers first. Many times we get so caught up in looking at the mountain that we walk right into the quicksand. My hope is that you keep your focus on the stars and the ground.

Realizations

"Spread your knowledge like leaves falling from a tree. That is your job."

One of the pet peeves I have is when an elderly person speaks of the past as though there is no future. There is no one on this earth that loves to hear of the past than I do, because it keeps me grounded and it teaches me many lessons. Not only that, but it makes for good conversation. I see new stories created by the HLTs, but I only hear the same old ones from the LLTs. Stop dwelling on your past conquests and create new ones. The past has given you the experience that you need to build something more; so build it. Your past has given you a taste of life, so keep tasting.

I mentioned earlier about my uncle who kept working even when he was very sick. He kept working because it is what kept him going. It is the challenge of his work and the "still living" part that fueled his fire, not the money.

I have a few questions to those elderly who are reading this. First, what are you going to do when you retire? What reason do you have to get out of bed? Why have you quit being prosperous just because you are retired? Don't you think you have something to give that can enrich others? Don't you think you have the obligation to give back to those who have helped you? Don't you think it's time to help others? Don't you think you have something to offer others? You have so much experience stored in that wonderful brain of yours, please do not waste it. I am so amazed at the knowledge each elder has that I visit. Each has their own expertise. They all have an abundance of information and knowledge that they have gathered through the years.

I drank coffee with my father and a few other gentlemen for the last thirty years and still do today. I am amazed that I can bring up issues in my own life for any subject and usually there is one out of the group that is familiar with that subject. Experience is your gift, use it.

Teaching is your job; do it. Your life is in front of you, go for it. That is what a HLT elder does and is. Follow me into the real world of an elder HLT and I will show you what I mean.

Entering the Real World

One day I was drinking coffee with one of my older gentlemen friends. In the conversation about his trips to see his wife in assisted living, he looked at me with that glare of intelligence and said, "I think it is time for me to stop driving so much." After we had a short conversation about limiting his driving, I took some time to analyze what had just taken place. I have had nothing but respect for this gentleman, because he always handled himself with a lot of class. However, after this, I put him on a whole new level in terms of HLT. Here is a man who deals in reality and understands that his actions may hurt him and others. This is a man who knows his words and his admittance to his physical changes could reduce his independence. He accepts that and in that acceptance he has made his world and the world of others safe around him. Most people go kicking and screaming when it comes to taking away their privileges. Most of the time, it is a selfish act. In all my years, I have never witnessed someone so strong in terms of dealing with reality. We think of people who do things for others, and it is visual. We acknowledge it, because it can be seen. But a HLT does things because it is the right thing to do. No one sees it. No one is around to cheer. No one is around to care—just the HLT and the truth. If I become half the man this man has become, I will create a lot of great trickle down events in my life. A trickle down is wrapped in honor because it is unselfish. Realizing and taking action is paramount.

All my friend has to do is use all of his God-given mental sharpness to come up with alternatives to maintain his freedoms and I know he will. Awareness was the only tool needed from his toolbox to save his life or the life of someone else.

There are also other types of safety awareness. How about the simple tasks that we take for granted, like climbing a ladder? I know of two friends who have died by falling off a five-foot ladder and sustaining life-ending injuries. Did you absorb that first part? They died from falling off a five-foot ladder? They lived on this earth for eighty-plus years and fell off a ladder and perished. As I write those words, I am sick to my stomach. They tore their families apart for something that could have been prevented so easily.

Another friend I knew fell from her porch, because the wind was so strong and her legs were so weak and because of that combination of events it lead to a broken hip bone, surgery, six months in assisted living then because of inactivity, eventually she passed on into eternity. She was going to get her hair done and was not going to be stopped. Well, she was stopped. I only bring up these sad stories to wake you up so there are no more sad stories to tell. I care about you too much. Safety should be your one and only concern. There was an abundance of safety options for both of those tragedies I mentioned, but pride and stubbornness overruled common sense and safety, and the tragedies won. The LLTs won over the HLTs and the prize was death. Think about that for a moment, and please argue with me if you can. I challenge you. We have just experienced real life events and they happen every day. My friend, the HLT, was aware of life and saw his life from above and took action to prevent bad happenings.

The last two examples were also my friends. However, they were not thinking and not aware of the dangers and paid the ultimate price. So did their families. A HLT would have dropped the pride and had someone hold the ladder or, better yet, had someone else do it. My other friend simply could have looked at the conditions and realized she was not stable, weighed the good and bad options, and stayed home that day. Yes, life is that simple, if you think ahead. I believe I have ruffled your feathers. Now let me help you build mountains. Use your awareness of dangers to keep you safe, so that you can get to the mountains. Once you have destroyed or outsmarted the negatives, it is time to climb the mountain.

I have spent my whole career in the service end of the oil industry. I am absolutely amazed at the passion some of these pioneers have for their job and I use the term job very loosely. I know several eighty-plus-year-old men still investing and drilling and they do not need the money.

The majority of the human race would say, "Go sit on a beach and relax you fool. I believe that the ones who do not follow their passions are the fools. I have seen the greatest of men and women mentally deteriorate due to sitting on the beach, so to speak. It is your job as a HLT elder to give the gift of your mind and experiences to the next generation. It is your job to set the example of building mountains, or simply giving back. There is so much knowledge in a mind for you to keep it to yourself. This is the biggest waste and the worst mental tragedy that I can think of. Do not keep your past knowledge within you. Pass on the baton to the next generation.

I have two very special friends of mine who donate their time as volunteers and run various church events. I believe their life is full, due to their gift of spirit, knowledge, and time. They follow the unselfish rule that a HLT possesses. What they give, I believe they receive tenfold. Their passion is to give. What is your passion? Make it your new job and go to work. A LLT will stop living. They will make excuses for their inability to chase their passion. The HLT will realize that even though the going will be slower and in some cases rougher, they know it will be more rewarding when they get there. A HLT will do things like create an advisory team to help companies get started, just for fun. They will organize trips and clubs, just so that they can stay sharp and involved in life. They will most likely bring others into their exciting world. Then that excitement will spread like wild fire to others. They can then feel great because they changed the lives of others for the better.

An elderly woman goes to that higher place and realizes that time has weakened her physically, but declares, "You will not beat me." She looks around the house and seeks ways to make her life more secure, like having a hand rail installed on her porch. She laughs because she won that battle. An elderly couple decides that it is getting a little too risky to be driving long distances. Their safety and the safety of others is a factor, so they seek options. They come up with two plans: Take a bus or seek out someone who is going to the same place. They make them an offer they cannot refuse like, they drive and the older couple pays for the hotel or the food. They have won!

And just to let Old Man and Old Woman Time know that they cannot be beat, they hold hands wherever they go. This is to symbolize that their strength as a couple is lasting and that they will continue to mentally challenge any force against them like they have for the last fifty years. Once again, they laugh. An older lady lives in a town with no relatives and needs a little added security. She seeks out a Christian family on the block and asks if they would call her once a day just to make sure everything is all right. For doing that she offers to cook their Thanksgiving turkey for them. Her resources are low, but her experience of cooking is enormous. Everyone wins and problem solved.

Are you making a one-hundred mile trip, but you are unsure if you can make it in one day? Take two days. It is ok, since you are retired.

Having problems paying your medical bills? Rent a room in your home.

Having a hard time remembering daily details? Buy a pound of sticky notes. (I use them every day, just so I do not forget what I probably will remember.) I thought of these ideas on my own in five minutes; you can too. Go above your life and see the problems and potential problems, think outside the box, and solve them.

One last example to leave you with: An older gentleman farmer I briefly knew had a stroke. His passion was farming. After a stroke that left him partially paralyzed, he hired a young lady that was familiar with the farm life and was out of a job. She took him to coffee, she took him to the store, and then she took him to the tractor, helped him on it, and let him go. My guess is that most LLTs in this situation would have given up on life, because the physical wall was too high to climb over. What the HLT does differently is realize that all walls run out somewhere. If you use your mind, you can eventually go around the wall, not over it. Money that he did have could not help keep his passion directly, but the money he had along with his mind created a solution to pay for the help to get him back to his passion.

"Strengthen your foundation physically by holding hands. Strengthen your foundation mentally by asking for help in seeking solutions to your ever changing issues."

The Challenge

To all of my elderly friends, with all the respect that you deserve, I must also challenge you. I challenge you to realize your mind is much stronger and more resourceful than your body. I challenge you to remember that your experiences and your knowledge of life is too powerful to let the simplest tasks and obstacles win the battles. I challenge you to go above your life and look down and come to terms with where you are in your life. Dare life, and create resources all around you to slow down the circle of life. I challenge you to drop your pride and use your mind to solve all of life's issues. If not on your own, ask others to help with your solutions. I dare you to say to Old Man Time, "I will create a team to fight you when you want to take my spirit." I challenge you to wake up every day and say, "What mountain can I build today?" Do not say, "I cannot, because of these reasons…" Say, "I can, because of these reasons…" Most importantly, I urge you to think of the dangers that await you, come up with a safer plan, and then laugh, because you are not a statistic, but a HLT.

The Higher Level View

You have seen a lifetime of failures and successes. I believe you will agree with me when I say those failures were due to a lack of the simple art of thinking. Your years of experience have taught you to be aware of the things in life that can harm or destroy who you are. There is one thing in your toolbox that no one else has and that is experience and the memory of those lessons. Now is the time to be the leader of life. Do not be the one who causes the trickle down of bad happenings. You taught your children to be responsible, now it is your turn to walk the walk of leadership. Show them how much better things work out when planning and awareness are common factors in your life. Do not forget to share that with them and plant that seed of thought. That is your job. Growing up, I remember it wasn't just the words that my elders said, it was their actions and the lessons they shared with me. Those were my greatest gifts. They made me a better person.

If you are a HLT, teaching by example requires self-empowerment. First, you do the right things. A HLT lives there and teaches from there, a higher place. I would like to thank you for doing your part in building the moral and mental foundation to make this world a better place. You have created life and your job as a HLT is to never stop teaching, not ever!

Chapter Eleven: HLT on Business Theory

The Art of the Deal, HLT-Style

"Business is about people, not money."

HAVE YOU ASKED yourself why you started your business in the first place? This is a great question. Did you start your business in order to supply a need or service for the public? Or was it to become successful and live the American dream? Both are valid reasons. Let's see if I can read your original thinking. You were going to play by all the rules and lead your people to success. You were going to treat your employees better than you were ever treated as an employee. You were going to listen to your employees, unlike your previous employer did. Most importantly, you were going to give customers what they wanted: great service, great attitude, and the respect they deserve.

Well, do you still have the same spirit you had when you started? Most likely, you do not. Time made you complacent. I see this in almost every business. The most successful companies in the world never forgot about two important things: their employees and their customers. That sounds simple, but the fact is they have been forgotten.

Past generations of companies used to pride themselves on customer service and quality of work—the customer comes first. Take care of the customer and the customer will take care of you. These businesses were built by HLTs and at no time did they stray off course.

These principals are taught HLTs on the first day employees show up for work. Focus on these principals and a new HLT is born. Then your company will become more solid or a new future great company will be born.

The greatest business has a leader who never forgot about the simplicity of that business theory. Treat the customer like you want to be treated if you were the customer. A great leader will remind their employees to live by that philosophy until it becomes second nature. Not only that, but a great leader will teach employees what their contribution and customer service can do for them. Focus on one thing and one thing only: the customer.

Business is simple: make money. Where most business theories go wrong is the selfishness that is allowed to grow within the company. It is also the lack of awareness of the customers' needs and the lack of focus to fill those needs. There are generally just two components—buyers and sellers. In every facet of business, there should be an "everyone wins" attitude and a middle ground, so all partners succeed.

Two tools needed in all forms of business are pre-thought and communication. The only way to be a HLT in business is to see both sides of the deal. The ultimate HLT business mind is where a middle ground is created and everyone wins. I protest the books that are written where the mindset is always a one-way win in the negotiation world. The problem with that theory is that if someone wins, then someone has lost, right? The art of the deal should be when everyone gets something for their effort. I understand those types of books are successful in terms of money, but that sounds a little selfish to me, doesn't it to you? Well, that is not what a HLT is all about. HLTs are unselfish. A HLT rises above all situations and creates a format where all can win.

If you are selling a car, don't you usually ask for a little more than you will actually take for the car? Sure, you do. That was the way you are taught—to try and beat the other person. If you are purchasing a car, isn't your intention to get the car for less? That is also the way we are taught. If you win, I ask you once again, what was lost? The true HLT leader and the true HLT business person see the bigger picture. The selfish short-term win has most definitely hurt any chance of long-term success, because your customer or your adversary in the deal leaves feeling defeated. You have reduced your chance of overall success since the transaction will probably be a one-time shot. As I mentioned earlier, you now must go above your business theory and see the whole picture, see your place, see your people, see your vision, and see your customer.

This is where most business leaders have a problem. They do not look at their business from different views. The two most important views are the view of the client and the view of the employee. It is the simplest concept known to man, so why are there so many unsatisfied customers? Why do we see so many flaws in businesses?

Many business people have lost their focus or have not been taught to focus on what is important—the customer and their own success or fulfillment. I have seen business owners so intent on the numbers that they forgot about the customers. All they had to do is get out from behind the calculator long enough to shake the hands of the people who made the calculator ring—their customer and their employees. More important than money is earning loyalty from your customers and employees. That is more powerful than all the books ever written. Plus, it will make the register ring.

If you are going to be a HLT, and build this loyalty and respect, you need to go to the level that creates awareness. As a customer, you want service. You want to feel good and you want to be pampered and understood. As customers, we all are naturally critics. There is a metamorphosis that happens when you own your own business. We forget about the view we were just in, the view of the customer. A HLT looks at his own business through the eyes of his customers. It is that simple. Most people would say that it is common sense. Welcome to the world of the HLT.

I will bet that everyone in business believes they are taking care of their customers. Only until you have looked through the eyes of your customers and have seen what they see and feel what they feel will you be a HLT.

Entering the Real World

Let me start by giving you a few examples of real-life situations. These events happened to me in same restaurant on different trips. While my wife and I were eating in a buffet-style restaurant we go to about five times a year, I noticed an area where the servers come out from the kitchen. It happens to be in the middle of where the patrons return with their full plates. It is a blind corner for each. I am not sure why anyone would design the area in that way. On several occasions, I noticed close calls between patrons and servers. I asked one of the servers about the awkward situation. She said she was nervous every time she walked out. So as a HLT student, I decided to see if I could make things better for all. I contacted the manager and pointed out the situation. He agreed that it was an awkward situation.

On the next trip, I noticed that a mirror had been placed above the corner so the servers could see if anyone was coming. The problem was solved because of awareness—unfortunately mine, not theirs. Now I could pat myself on the back for instigating the change, but this is not what this book or I am about. The question is what do think about that incident? I personally am very disturbed by that event. First, the architect did not take into consideration client or employee safety. Also, the manager should have taken the step I did and focused on the problem. It had appeared to me that the manager was more concerned about looking good than in serving the needs of his employees and customers, even though his company was looking at a potential lawsuit several times a day. A HLT would have observed the problem before it became an issue and fixed it. By reading this, are you now visualizing your place of business from a different view? If so, welcome to the land of the HLT.

The second situation occurred at the beverage service area of this establishment. This particular bar area had seating around and along the bar. There was no place to walk up and order a beverage without squeezing in between two patrons. This awkwardness, to say the least, made for a very uncomfortable situation. I sought out the manager and explained the customer's point of view. Soon after, a planned remodel included a walk up area for patrons. A LLT manager would not notice the need. The HLT manager would have noticed and addressed the need.

During the morning buffet at the same buffet-style restaurant, there is a gentleman that makes an omelette to your request. You have two choices: You can wait and create your own omelette or you can proceed through the rest of the buffet. However, the omelet ordering station is right in front of the buffet line. To begin your journey through the breakfast buffet, you must ask several people if they are waiting in line in the omelette line or the buffet line. What is the big deal, you ask? They are all in the same line. Everyone wonders if they should ask or push through the crowd. It makes for an awkward situation. As a practicing HLT, I could not believe management had not addressed the problem. Once again poor design created this issue and there was no need for it. What is equally amazing is how easy the problem was to solve. My suggestion was to put up a small sign a few feet back from the beginning of the buffet line instructing those who are not waiting for an omelet to move forward to the buffet line. That last solution took me about two minutes to solve, only because I have felt the frustration because I am a customer. I focused on the issue because I care. I solved the issue because that is what a HLT does.

A business that does not focus on customer service loses customers. Most hotel and restaurant owners I know have never sat down and eaten at their own restaurant or slept in their own hotel beds.

The restaurant I have been talking about has since remodeled their buffet area and it is beautiful. Guess what did not change. You got it. The frustrating buffet area. Beautiful bricks without customer service are just beautiful bricks, not a productive restaurant.

The next two business theory examples I would like to share with you are not as much as the art of the deal, but the art of the people. Bankers and car dealers both get somewhat of a bum rap when it comes to dealing. Some people think they make a huge amount of money on a deal, but that is just not true. They earn their paycheck one business deal at a time, just like anyone else. They are earning a living just like you and me. If you do not like the price of the car, simply don't buy it. If you do not like the terms of the loan, don't borrow. You have the power, so quit blaming them for trying to make a living. That is not where I am going with this theory, though. I just had to get that off my chest. Once again, business is about people, not numbers.

When I was inquiring about a newer vehicle, to my dismay the sales person never asked me about myself, my driving habits, my physical condition, my needs, or my wants. He just handed me a book about the various vehicles. I thanked him, walked out, and never went back. I made another attempt with another salesperson a few months later and it was a completely different experience. She showed me several vehicles, but never asked about me. She was a terrific salesperson in terms of making my wife and I feel good and certainly bent over backwards for us. But she did not ask the questions that would have saved us all a lot of time and trouble. For instance: Do you drive long distances? What are you willing to spend? Are you interested in new or used cars? If either salesperson had asked those questions, we could have narrowed things down to the right vehicle. Actually, we found the used one we purchased on their lot, looking on our own. If these questions were asked they would have given me the impression that I was their concern, not “the sell.”

I moved to my current bank because the last bank was treating me like a number. Well, I am not wealthy. However, I certainly am not a number. If I was, it should be number one. In fact all their patrons should be.

I am not mad at this bank—disappointed is a better choice of words. I used to know the bankers and tellers by name. I felt like I was walking into my own front door when I came in. I liked going inside rather than going through the drive through for two reasons: One, it felt good to be welcomed; and two, the personnel got to know me so I didn’t have to worry about anyone trying to use my name or cash my checks. I did not mind paying a little extra for a loan, because I wanted to do business with my friends. That is why they were a great bank. Times change and I understand that nothing stays the same, but their service and their special treatment of customers should. Once, when I went in to inquire about a small home equity loan with one of their new loan officers, she handed me a pamphlet with the information on it. I must say that it certainly was a pretty pamphlet. However, she did not ask me one question about myself or my wife or our goals or dreams. She did not want to test my intelligence level with any type of probing questions. She did not seem to care if our family, though not wealthy, had deep roots in the area. She did not ask me what I did for a living or what my hobbies were or whether I had a dream to build a mountain—well, that last part might be a little dramatic. To make a long story short, I went somewhere else where they asked me those questions and, yes, I will probably build my mountain with someone else.

That is good business. Is it yours? Have you lost customers because of the lack of details and care? This bank did, and that is a fact. I was the customer and that is why I did not get a loan there.

A HLT loan officer would ask the questions for one simple reason: They care. They are interested in you and they want to help you build the bridges over the river to get to your mountains and they are glad to do it with you.

Now let us go a little deeper yet. I talked about the numbers and they are important, but it is the customer's mentality which should be screened before the numbers. I know of two businesses in town that I thought would fail because of the mentality of their owners, and they did fail. One built a new, very large and very expensive building for essentially the same clientele. Nothing really changed except for higher payments. The second built new structures replacing the old ones which did not add any revenue at all, but it did add—you guessed it—higher payments and higher taxes. Both banks loaned them money and both companies failed. They failed because of the owners and bankers mentality, not the business. The thought process in charge of the numbers is gold. There is no way you can increase your debt load without increasing your costs—that is a simple business mentality—but it was overlooked by those in charge of the financial strings and the owners of these two businesses.

Numbers speak for themselves anyway. What is overlooked is the intelligence level of those spending or borrowing the money. Are they smart enough to handle the money and the challenge of the new investment? It is all about intelligence.

The next example is one that I have yet to understand about business people in general. It is called the box. We have all heard about the box. The LLTs have six sides to their box with no opening. The ALTs have a lid, but they open it only when necessary. The HLT knows the box is good in one respect, because it sits on the ground—which represents a standard for a strong business foundation. The only difference is that their HLT box has no top. It opens to the heavens with thoughts like angels wings. Your HLT mind must look for every edge and option in every avenue of business, not just the norm. Everyone I know talks a good game, but when it actually comes to stretching their mind, they pull back to that familiar territory: The standard.

I once had an older piece of property I wanted to sell. We decided to go through the normal procedures to sell our rental property. I set up a time with a realtor friend of mine to look at the property. The ball was rolling, and I was excited that we would all be successful when the day was done—a win-win. To my surprise, my realtor was more interested in the negatives of the home than the positives. I agree that since it was an older home, there were more negatives than positives. The price he was talking about for the sale of the home definitely clashed with mine, because I knew there were people out there that would like it because the payments would be cheaper than renting in our town. We could not agree on that principle. It is like the restaurant buffet example all over again. Sometimes you have to lead people to a better place.

I looked in "his box" of highlighting the negatives not the positives, and I did not like what I saw. So I decided to take the lid off the traditional box and lead people to my house on my own. I calculated what the payments would be on a thirty year fixed rate and put it in an advertisement in the paper: "You can own a home for (x) amount of dollars per month which would be cheaper than renting." When people called me about the house the first thing they asked me was, "What do you mean I can own a house for x dollars a month which is cheaper than rent?" I told them the financial details of the loan and the potential of the house. Then I asked them about their situation and found out they could do some of the extra work it needed. I told them all the things that were done to the house that they would not have to do, such as new flooring, kitchen, paint, and water heater. I highlighted the fact that these items would save them money in the long run. I told them if we did not go through a realtor, I would even give them a discount off the total price. My wife and I sold the house in three days. That way of thinking will not fit in a box, the wings are too big. Sounds like I am bragging, doesn't it? Really, I am not. I am advertising HLT thinking, no box included. An interesting fact is that since I had placed that ad in the paper, I have noticed other similar ads of the same nature. That makes me feel good because I helped others open their box and let their minds fly.

The last portion of this real world HLT business party is a stew of examples of common sense in the business world. Just to keep the stew of thoughts boiling and to free your ideas into the sky, I am going to ask some questions. First: If you were advertising your restaurant, would you show the cook preparing the food with his bare hands? In most advertisements, they do. I do not eat at those restaurants. Second: In a restroom facility, does it make sense to have the wash basins on the opposite wall as the blow dryer or towels? Well, I know of a very large discount center that does this. I see a potential lawsuit coming from a wet floor, don't you? Third: Have you ever asked the question, "Should I send my client one copy or two?" I hear that question a lot. Why would you not send them two? All three of those questions are simple to answer. Of course you should not show a cook using their bare hands to prepare a meal. Do not show it in an advertisement, and don't allow it to take place in real life. Also, it doesn't make sense to have your patrons walk across the floor with dripping wet hands and risk injury and a lawsuit. Why would you not give your clients what they need? These simple business-minded lapses can cost you clients. Is that what you want? It is time to wake up and pay attention to details and ask questions in reverse, as a patron might ask them. Do you want to eat what someone has touched? Do you want to slip on a wet floor and get hurt? Wouldn't you rather have two copies of a transaction instead of just one for your files? It is that simple. If your business is failing, maybe it is because you are failing your business. Think about it.

The Challenge

I now challenge all business minds to stop talking the talk and start walking the walk. If you claim that you are a HLT, then it is time to step up and play the part. I can talk this way because I have proof that I am right, and you are my witness. I do not go to the some of these places I have talked about, and that is real. Your memory of your customers' experiences in business is the truth. Walk into any establishment and open your eyes. Usually there will be an obvious problem that needs to be corrected. As you walk in, do so as though you are looking through the eyes of a client. Walk through your front door as your customers do, rather than through the back door. Sit down and focus. Be your own customer. Recognize the flaws in your own place. Eat your own food. Listen for laughter. Notice the service. Go into the restroom and look for issues that relate to cleanliness and safety. For example, is the trash can next to the door? I personally do not want to wash my hands, dry them, and then touch the door handle that the previous guy touched—who did not wash his hands. Do you?

The biggest challenge is ask patrons how they feel about your restaurant. Do they have any ideas that would make their evening out more pleasurable? Observe what the employees go through on a daily basis. Feel their pain, and do something about it.

If you are a car dealer or a banker, get to know your customers. That is what your business is all about. It is not about cars or money; it is about people.

Boxes were made for containment. You can keep your mentality in a closed and comfortable environment if you wish, and when your mind gets full, I also suppose you can just empty out your box. Or you can open the lid and let the world be your new box—no boundaries, and a new way of thinking that can go into infinity. The words will flow and spawn new ideas, but always carry the box—a great foundation that all businesses need. Wake up and take a walk around your business. See your business, listen to your business, seek out potential problems, and solve them.

The Higher Level View

On two separate flights I sat next to two different men. The first man had been in real estate for twenty-plus years. He told me of a situation where his tenants were less than kind to his place, but mostly out of habit, not spite. I had used this out-of-the-box technique of mine on several occasions, which I gladly shared with him. It was the idea of an incentive package for his tenants. If the property was taken care of, he would deposit a small amount of funds into an account each month and when they moved out, an inspection would be implemented, and the money left over—after repairs—would be theirs, along with the deposit. It works with some people in the right environment. What that plan does is create a partnership of sorts. Their lack of thought process or their lack of respect for my property might be overpowered by the reward to come. It has worked for me, and that is the truth. He said he had never heard of anything like that in his twenty years of real estate. My short-term opinion of this gentleman was that he was an ALT. He had potential, but was mentally stagnate. I wish I knew how that advice worked for my new friend. I truly hoped it worked well.

My first impression of the next gentleman I met was that he was a HLT. He told me he owned a fast food business, but he said he treats his place differently than a normal fast food chain. He runs it like a normal business, meaning he does not use multi-interchanging, part-time people. He hires full-time workers who have a stake in the company. He said he pays them well, and trains them even better. He gives them responsibility and a dream. He teaches them how to be good business people, and that requires taking care of your customers needs, and always calls for you to be friendly and courteous. At first I was a little skeptical, because I always try to seek the truth in every situation. I realize most individuals believe they are doing a good job; it is an ego thing. This individual's business was located in a city about two hours drive from my hometown. It turned out to be about a block away from the hospital where my wife had an appointment that day. I was going to have my sweet, skeptical revenge, as I walked in the front doors and was anticipating the disappointment I would witness. Well, my sweet revenge was disappointed, because by every account—except for the fact that I really did not care for the type of food he served—he was right. It was a fast food place, but I was greeted when I came in. The employees were very friendly. They were always cleaning, and they even came over while I was eating to ask if I needed anything. This was a fast food restaurant, and they asked me if I needed anything! Can you believe it? I stayed for about an hour and was amazed at the sight. It was clear that a HLT was in charge of what I considered a breeding ground of future HLTs. I asked where my new friend was, since I knew this particular place was where he had his office. They told me he had been playing in a golf tournament all week in Arizona, which was where he had been when I met him on the plane. He must have been a great teacher and leader with faith in his people to be gone that long. The mice weren't playing when the cat was away, apparently because they respected the cat, and they had a stake in the cheese of success. They also were doing their job, because it is what HLTs do. Even though no one is watching, it is who they are inside. I believe that my new friend, who I have never seen since the plane trip, is a business HLT.

To finalize this HLT summary, you must look for the edge in your business. It could be the food, the service, the easy layout, or the friendly, self-motivated people. Nice try, you were going to pick just one, weren't you? It takes more than one thing or one person; it takes everyone, everyday. That is a HLT business theory. Now go do it!

Chapter Twelve: The HLT Manager

"Focus on the solution using the employee, not focusing on the problem of the employee."

IF EINSTEIN WORKED for you, would he or she still be Einstein? Wouldn't it be wonderful if Einstein did work for you? I am not suggesting that there are a lot of Einsteins out there or that they work for you, but it does make you think, doesn't it? If it made you think, then you have just visited the land of the HLT.

Let's imagine that a man works for the second biggest company in a particular sector. His ideas to improve on the business are quickly extinguished by the LLT management. This particular employee has had enough. He throws his financial security out the window and quits. He approaches the biggest company in that field, gets hired, and within two years, he is in charge of his own division. The next year, he turns around the stagnate division and it becomes the top division of the company. I wonder why that company is the top company in the land. I will tell you why. They, the ownership and the management, believe in making everyone as good as they can be. The leaders are not selfish. They promote HLTs and are excited by it, because it pulls everyone up to another level.

If you are a HLT manager, then you are the gatherer of minds first. Then you are the leader of the problem solving or problem preventing task force. If you are a HLT leader, then you will never put a ceiling of thought anywhere in your company. You must promote creativity and teamwork. This builds an excitement in the workforce like no other, and gives your employees a sense of purpose. This will be extremely difficult if you do not prepare yourself with the mindset that all can be satisfied in your company under your leadership. Selfishness has no place in this leadership role. The trickle-down theory that we previously discussed is now more apparent than ever. You are on the stage, whether you want to be or not.

The company will be exactly how you present it. If you are negative, the trickle down will be ugly. If you are positive, the company will flourish. If you are smart, intelligence will soar. If you lack common sense, you will be riddled with problems. If you promote service, your company reputation will be that of service. If you are selfish, your company will decline by that spirit alone. It is the trickle down of life, and it all starts with you. Being a nice person is not always the right answer, because people take advantage of nice people. Employees can get soft and complacent. Being tough is not always the right answer, because you are looked at as a dictator and that brings resentment. So what is the answer? What is the magic that makes a successful company run smoothly? What makes people live up to their potential and creates harmony in the workplace? It is activating the potential that your wonderful beautiful mind holds. It is the ability of the manager's mind to go above his workplace or, better yet, the effort of the manager to go above the workplace and see the whole picture first. His or her business theory should include the success and happiness of employees and the satisfaction of clients. See employees for what they truly represent, and for what is in their spirit. Realize where you were just a few years ago and the mindset that you had, and search for the potential in everyone. If someone does not have leadership abilities, accept that. However, treat them like they do.

The Self-examination of a HLT Manager

If anyone in your company says, "I love my job, but…,"most likely you are not a good manager.

To become a great HLT manager, you must create your reality, and ask yourself some tough questions. By doing this, you will open up your own mind to the unselfish answers. By this random self-questioning, you will stir up your own awareness to make sure you are not the problem with your company. Since the top is where you are, you must represent internal strength. These questions will help. Go through them and answer truthfully. Afterward, we will address a few of them with a higher level thought process.

1. Do I keep my employees under my own ceiling of thought?
2. Am I, and have I been firm, fair, and consistent?
3. Do I set guidelines and back them up with action, and do I mean what I say?
4. Do I communicate our objectives and keep everyone focused on the goal?
5. Do I let everyone in my company with an opinion have a chance to be heard?
6. Have I looked at the positive and the negative aspects of my decisions before reacting?
7. Do I leave my self-pride at the front door when I come to work?
8. Have I looked through the eyes of my employees?

9. Have I looked through the eyes of my customers?
10. Have I shown appreciation for the work the employees have done?
12. Do I wish things would be better or do I make them better?
13. Do I create the trickle down of positive attitudes and expect the same from my employees?

Here is the ultimate question in the HLT self examination: Have I searched every avenue of possibilities to create all possible future problems and gathered every mind in my company to solve all of these future problems? I bet you haven't. I bet you wait for the problems to happen before you work on the solutions. That is normal, so I do not blame you for that mentality. Your HLT cannot consist of normal thinking behavior. In the HLT business world, you must be thinking at all times about the next potential problem. Remember, we are going above your workplace. We are looking down and focusing on each situation, all employees, their needs and wants, strengths and weaknesses.

With the direction of the company, we can then begin to see potential problems that can occur. With the powerful tool called communication, we can solve most issues before they become a problem. That is what a HLT manager does and is.

The story I brought up at the beginning of this chapter is a sad, but true example of many businesses. If only the manager would have gotten out of his self-absorbed world and focused on his employees, he would have seen a gem or an Einstein. He would have seen an employee who actually wants to succeed in his company. He would have seen an opportunity for growth and excitement and a chance to release some employees to take on more responsibility and to have better lives. The trickle down should have been a positive one where all involved win, but because he did not use the awareness tool, he and his company lost a potential Einstein or, at the least, a dedicated employee who wants the company to succeed.

Let us now break down a few of those reflection questions and keep the theme running. Remember, the top is always where you are, not where you think you are. Only until you see inside yourself will changes begin on the outside and begin the trickle down of great happenings in your company. Let us analyze some of these questions and stimulate your management brain. Remember, if just one of these is being neglected, you will start the trickle down of bad vibrations to your company, and it will be your fault.

1. Do I keep my employees under my own ceiling of thought?

Well, do you? Do you believe that just because you have a title, you are the only person that has a brain? That was a little harsh. However, you probably believe you are smarter than the ones under you. Now, by that theory, before you became a manager, you were not smart enough to be a manager. By some divine intervention and a title, you are now a genius. I am not picking on you. I just want all managers to understand that it is not all about your mind. If an employee has some great ideas, your job is to explore those thoughts and, if possible, let this potential Einstein shine. His or her success is your success. That is the only way to look at management. Any other way will bring resentment and a trickle-down feeling to your employees. It will cause them to feel like you do not care. So, in their minds, why should they? A HLT looks at every tree (mind), because all the trees (minds) together create the beautiful blooming forest which is called a successful company.

The Challenge

I challenge all managers to call a meeting first thing tomorrow morning and ask every employee their opinion about your company. Leave the ego at home. Work on a question and answer format and let all your employees have a say. Tell them your vision for the company and ask them to help. Create a format where you listen to their opinions about all the potential problems that can derail this vision. By using this respectful method, you will see a sparkle in the eyes of every person in the room, because they will now feel a sense of purpose and feel like they are part of a team. You, as a HLT, will now feel like a true leader and that little ego we all have will turn into pride. What will happen next is that your more reserved employees will spring to life with thoughts. Great personalities and future leaders will now appear before your eyes and the greatest thing will be that you, as a HLT, did it. You brought your company to life. You created the trickle down of great happenings, and did not put out dreams. Now, when you let everyone out of the meeting, listen and feel what you have accomplished. You have changed lives. Your employees will go home and have a smile on their face that their spouse has never seen before, yes, the trickle down of a HLT, the top is where you are. Do it!

The Higher Level View

From your new vantage point, can you see where some minds want to go? Can you see the potential in some, and hopefully, all of your employees? Can you see the ones that are being stifled, their dreams being put out because of your limited thought process? Can you see where you have been keeping everyone down instead of bringing them up so you look better? Let them push higher. Do not push them down, the results are so depleting. If ego is what you want, what a better way to build one than by building an incredible team?

A HLT builds dreams for everyone. LLTs only build up themselves. Because of you, tomorrow is going to be a new, inspiring day for you and your employees. Challenge their minds to anticipate potential problems and solve them. Inspire them to become better than you, and that will automatically inspire you to become a better leader, better person, and a better HLT.

2. Do I communicate our objectives? Do I set guidelines, and am I firm, fair and consistent?

This is a fairly simple formula for a HLT. However, this is where the fine line between taking charge and micromanaging is created. The communication part is easy if you are a communicator. If not, and most managers I know are not, this is where the trickle down of bad happenings are going to run wild. You have two choices if you are going to be a HLT manager. Give someone else the authority who can communicate well and back them up, or get trained to be a better communicator. You have no other options. A HLT looks for the best possible solutions to the problem and prevents most problems from happening in the first place. If you are a terrible communicator, then you have become the problem in your company since you are the boss. No one will be able to rectify the situation that you have caused; they simply do not have the authority. HLT managers don't need to be the best at a certain job. They just need to find the best person suited for the job and communicate to them the vision. Why do managers of successful companies hire motivational speakers? Because motivation has become a need, and they do not have the tools to motivate. Also, they are smart enough to be aware of it. So they hire someone with that skill. If everyone in your company does not have the same vision and passion, then you have not done your job. You have not prevented the major problems in your company that will arise because of the lack of communication—yes, you. Do not blame others.

The manager is responsible for communication, no matter what means it takes to get this accomplished. The fine line between taking charge and micromanaging is using two simple solutions: One is staying focused on the ultimate goal and the other is your delivery of the request.

The fine line between dictatorship and micromanaging is keeping everyone focused and underscoring their importance in the company. If they feel their role is unimportant, then they will need to be pushed along in their job; they will feel micromanaged. On the other hand, if you speak directly, define your goals, and make them feel they are valuable to the vision, then you have created a team atmosphere. Those individuals will feel like they have some control over their lives and have added value to the company vision. Even when being told to perform a task, they will feel it is all right, because they are now doing their part in making the company a success. Their mind is now free to think and produce valuable ideas for the company. Employees may not be completely happy, but at least they will be more satisfied.

As a manager, make sure others stay on the course set by your company's objectives. It does not matter if you have a free spirit company or one that has a high liability attached. You must not bend the rules for one. You may change your company policy as a whole, but do not allow one to stretch the rules. If you do, then you will create disloyalty, back stabbing, gossip, and, most certainly, distrust. Your job, as a HLT manager, is to make the rules apply to all. If you do not, the trickle down of bad happenings will be created and you will not be able to reverse it. Firm, fair, and consistent is the only way to run your ship.

The Challenge

I challenge you today to look inside yourself and see situations that could have been improved upon, problems that could have been avoided, and ideas that could have been explored simply by communicating your company's vision. I challenge you to create your company vision from above and put guidelines in place to accomplish that vision. Let the team players see the whole picture. Give them direction, a goal, and a reason to give you one hundred percent. I want to challenge you to be firm, fair, and consistent with everyone in your company. That is the only way to keep unity and peace. Resentment grows out of unfairness. If a HLT stays consistent, he or she may change their direction, however, the team must move as a group. Inconsistency brings questions about leadership and turns into favoritism, which in turn breeds resentment. So, create your own awareness of your people and remember what it was like to be in their position when things were wrongly committed. How did you feel about that? A little resentful, maybe? Well, you are now a manager. Go to work and change it, HLT.

The Higher Level View

A lack of communication, an inability to set and follow through with guidelines, and a constant wavering on key principles become very clear from this higher new view. As you focus on these issues, you will most likely have a little inside turmoil. When your mind is open to what role you are playing, self-examination is a good thing. You are making sure you are not the problem. Are problems being created due to the lack of communication? Is a lack of communication causing procedure problems, meeting deadlines, or scheduling and planning issues? How about proper training or the lack thereof? The reason for doing the task at hand is extremely important. Knowledge of the goal and how the goal relates to success are paramount. A HLT manager makes sure everyone is told what the goals are and what each individual's responsibilities are to achieve those goals. Individuals are told how the process works, so everyone can be successful. They are told up front what will be expected to hold up their end of the deal. They are told how to excel and how to get help from existing team members. More importantly, they are given an avenue to express their ideas, goals, wants, and needs. Success can only happen if you look from above, then leave your higher view, go back down to earth, and take charge of the next meeting. Clear out the negatives that cause people to hold back instead of releasing, and then move on. A HLT sees the beauty in communication and the need for discipline, fairness, and consistency in the workplace. Without this foundation your company will regress.

3. Have I looked at all the positives and negatives in our decision-making process?

One of the most important leadership gifts you can give to your employees is the gift of unified pre-thought. You must create an atmosphere with your employees that consists of exploring all the worst-case scenarios and use all the minds at your disposal to solve each potential problem. You must create this atmosphere with the idea that there is no stupid question and no dumb ideas.

This question and mindset should be at the forefront of all meetings: If anything could go wrong, what would it be? Now, let's solve it now before it does happen." Too many times, higher-positioned people (not necessarily the HLT) forget how the nuts and bolts of an operation actually work. Perhaps technology has changed since they were in that position.

Why would you think you should know all the day-to-day problems and the answers to solve them? Sometimes, if you get too high, you cannot see the ground anymore. That is where most companies are built, and that is where the foundation is laid. Nothing is built from the top down. It must start at the bottom and work up. Before you make a management decision, check with your company's foundation—your employees.

They know your foundation better than you, so build from their opinions. The top is where you are, so you should see what the trickle-down effect is going to create at the bottom. A HLT will create only the best option for all by using all of his or her resources.

The Challenge

In every situation you face as manager, bring in all the parties involved. Create a solution-based atmosphere by seeking all the opinions of your employees and breakdown the good and bad scenarios that will be affected by that decision.

I promise you, you can still be the boss. You are just in charge of the process. By this simple act, you will create unity with all your people. You will give them all self-worth, because they helped with the solution-making process. By doing so, you will have created a more loyal team, which can only help you and your company in the long run. Even if you are selfish, man, you look good with good results. This is what a HLT does. They realize they are not labeled a manager, but essentially they are a leader. A leader will make the effort to look at all the best- and worst-case options along with soliciting all opinions for the good of the whole team.

The Higher Level View

The beautiful view of a HLT is where they see and feel empowerment, because they put out the effort to create solution-minded people. The HLT view creates a wonderful world most LLTs would say is fantasy, because HLTs are anticipating problems that do not yet exist. So why, they ask, should we go to the time and trouble to solve a problem that doesn't exist? Good point, or is it?

Is it better to solve a potential problem now while you have a positive, supportive team environment or to wait until the problem has disrupted progress or destroyed the company? Preventive measures will not cause a negative trickle-down effect. Some would say adversity creates intelligence and strength. However, that is too close to an excuse for me. The only entity that separates the two is effort. Why not create the probable problems and solve them? Then there are no more problems and your company is free to grow. You have controlled the company's destiny. Waiting on the problem is what victims and LLTs do. If everything is going well in a company, generally it is because the leader is using the pre-thought to stop the trickle down of bad happenings, not because they are lucky or because it is easy. A HLT makes a difficult job look easy, because they are thinking about all the potential problems all the time. Are you now prepared to do what it takes to be a HLT manager? If so, take another look at yourself and your company, and go to work.

4. Do I look through the eyes of my employees?

"I love my job, but...," I wish I had a nickel for every time I heard that line. Your employees could be happy and your workplace could hum if you attempted to explore your employees' wish list. I do not expect all your employees' wishes to come true. However, your success is in the effort. Most people do not realize what they have until it is gone. That sounds like a cheesy love story, but it is true in the business world, not a fantasy. I have witnessed great teams fall apart only because managers could not see the potential in front of them—a high performance, high intelligent work force with loyalty. What was their downfall? It was because the management refused to listen to the issues of the employees, because they did not have the tools themselves to solve the problems. Generally, the requests are small, but left alone, they build into mountains. You cannot stick your head in the sand. You must listen to what they say and how they feel. Seek their solutions. That is your job. Again, handling and preventing problems is your job. You must go to that higher level and use your awareness and communication tools to seek the solutions for your employees' happiness. I have talked to many employees that had issues and their manager had no clue there was an issue.

If you are a manager, whose fault is it? It is yours. You should have asked and cared. I would rather have a pat on the back and respect than to be given another dollar. A dollar, I will spend, but respect will give me the gratification to succeed.

The Challenge

The only vision you should see, internally speaking, is from your employees' eyes, because they are the ones looking at you for leadership and appreciation. What did you want your manager to be like before you were a manager? Firm? Yes, because it kept things fair. Fair? Yes, because it showed you they would give anyone willing to work hard a shot at improving themselves. Consistent. Yes, because it showed that your leader was strong enough to stick with and back up who was right. Ask yourself if you are the HLT manager that you wanted to look up to. Well, are you?

The Higher Level View

Do you remember how it felt before you were a manager? Do you remember co-workers doing things they should not do and the boss looking the other way? Do you remember leaders making decisions that affected you? You were not given enough respect to be asked your opinion? How did you feel? Small and overlooked? Your mind was like a volcano, just waiting to explode with great and interesting ideas, but no one listened or asked. You were so into the company, you could see potential problems and you worked on the solutions, but no one cared.

Well, leader, if you go to the place of a HLT, then you will see these people. Let them speak. Let them be great. Give them a reason to come to work each day. You will be that unselfish HLT, and you will be the leader of a great company with great employees—a HLT manager.

5. Have I looked through the eyes of my customers?

You may go to any business school on the planet. You may study numbers, theories, and equations all you like, but I will put my money on a HLT any day against all of the elite graduates. If only they would go to that higher place we talk about, and see the most simplistic business theory of all—looking through the customers' eyes and asking, "How would I want to be treated?"

How many times have you walked into an establishment and were treated in a way that wasn't conducive to or structured to you, the customer? How did you feel? A HLT takes that feeling to a different level and says, "That will not happen at my place." That feeling you had should propel you to the next level. Once you do something about it, and look for those issues at your place, you have now become a HLT. If your mind remains without focus and you do not learn from your bad experiences in other businesses, then you are a LLT. I have witnessed restaurant owners that were dinning out in another restaurant and were running down their service. Soon after that incident, I tried their restaurant and do you know what? They should have kept quiet. Use lessons to become better. Learn from other people's mistakes, and go to work in your own backyard. Remember the manager who did not look through the eyes of his customers? Because of that lesson, other customers and I are now reluctant to patronize this establishment. A loyal customer is now lost. Remember that the word of mouth is powerful. You build a business one customer and one big mouth at a time. Or you can lose one customer by one big mouth at a time.

The Challenge

I now challenge you to walk into your own restaurant. Wait to be seated, order, look around, see the flaws, see the sunshine, see the workers, and the deadbeats. Listen to the music. See the places that need to be cleaned. See the eye sores in front of you. Do you feel like you would like to eat there? Is there laughter? Is there quiet? I challenge you to go through the buffet at the busiest time and feel how frustrating it is? If so, do something about it.

How about the service industry? When was the last time you made a courtesy call to your customers? Do you realize when they speak about their needs, that is now your new vision as a com pany? When customer X says, "You are doing me a great service, however I would like to see this happen," and your response is, "Here we go again, another demand," then you are a LLT manager. If your response is, "This is wonderful. If I can make this happen, I have just secured this client for some time to come," "Here is my edge," then you are a HLT. You are now controlling the success of your business—now and in the future. I challenge you to become this kind of HLT manager.

You must create and take charge of these business opportunities. Create being the key word. The company pays you to create opportunities for your company and your clients. It is a full-time job. There are no holidays. Your brain should never sleep. You must keep your employees happy. However, the only way to do that is to keep your customers happy. Do it tomorrow, and feel the empowerment of thinking.

The Higher Level View

This is a simple view to take. In fact, this is the perfect place to be selfish, if you need that release. We all do from time to time. It keeps us human. We are being selfish here in thought only because, in doing so, we are serving others. When you ask yourself how you would like to be treated, then you are solving issues you might have had with your customer. A HLT's view is very simple: Do not look at your customers, look *with* your customers. Your job, as a HLT manager, is to use your mind and melt it into the mind of your client. From then on, what makes them satisfied will also make you satisfied. Both will win. The customer will receive service and a little pampering, and the business will receive a loyal customer and success.

6. Have I trained my employees to look through the eyes of the customer?

Business is all about the customer; the rest is conversation. Training must be done right to succeed. Managers should focus on the customer, rather than just thinking, "What's in it for me." Unfortunately, employers make promises to their employees without seeing if they can satisfy the customer first. The mindset the manager should give to their employees is that if we give the customer what they need, then we will get what we want: The American Dream. You must give first, before you receive. Then, and only then, will both the buyer and seller win. A HLT sees the big picture and realizes how giving can produce receiving, and in that, they can continue giving. Now how does this happen? It is when you have the backbone and the commitment of a leader. It is when you teach this simple, but forgotten, philosophy to your employees. Show your employees how this different view of business can affect the bottom line for the company. If you do, you will have a positive team, eager to satisfy the customer. By showing them the big picture, you will encourage them to find ways to serve the customer better. In turn, this will light your company with passion and ideas.

The Challenge

I walked into a restaurant one day with my book work in hand, obviously looking to be seated in a quiet area in order to do some work. I specifically chose a time after 1:00 p.m. for my lunch, because I knew it would be quiet. The nice, personable hostess asked me if I wanted to be seated. "Absolutely," I said with a smile. I asked if I could have a corner booth for obvious reasons to the both of us. I was quick to thank her and proceeded with my plan to be creative and nourished. Just a few minutes later, I heard the joyous sounds of five children, and they were not looking for a nap. They were hungry and restless, and they were heading to the booth right next to me by the same hostess who had seated me. In fact, they bypassed many similar booths farther away. I could not get mad, for I did go to a public place. This is the chance you take, and I take full responsibility for that. My point is that a HLT manager would have taught his employees to be observant to the needs of their customers. Obviously, if there were no other options, it would have been ok. In this particular case, there were a lot of them. I was not thought of and I have never been back there for lunch. I work a lot on my lunch breaks, because my brain is in full gear. Now I patronize a place where I hope they will give me respect. In other words, I will never be back for lunch again at that restaurant. I am not mad at this restaurant or the server. I am just making a point to help your business. Customers go to a place for a reason, and they choose not go to places for a reason. You must make sure that when they get to your place, you take care of their reason. It is that simple. Was it the young hostess' fault? A little. I put more blame on the manager. He or she had a perfect opportunity to teach employees about respecting their patrons, but failed. So now I must challenge you to first know the difference between great and poor customer service, and then train your employees to know the difference, too. In this case, it did make a difference in their future, because I now go somewhere else for my working lunch.

The Higher Level View

I would love to tell you that managing is an easy chore, but it is not. I do know that in order to be a HLT manager, you must know business. You must be internally strong enough to stand up for what is right. Lead by that example, and never let weaker attitudes and business practices bring down your company's morale and success. The only way to make management happen is to raise the level of thinking to people who, in some cases, may not be used to that concept yet. I believe the answer is this: If you are at the higher level, do not try to drag them to your level kicking and screaming. Let them walk with you for a while. Let them absorb the feeling of responsibility. Take them to lunch at your place, and ask them to see what you see. Lead them to that higher Promised Land. Teach them what is in it for them if the clients are happy and the company is successful. That should get their attention. If not, you must let them go. Tell them how they can advance in your company if they break out of the pack mentally. Remember, your job as a HLT manager is to make the people as good as you are. That is the true unselfish spirit of a HLT.

7. Am I the manager who wishes it would be better or do I make them better?

Interesting question. I recall a friend who, for years, unloaded his work baggage on me every time we met. It was always the company's internal problems that ruined his day. One time, his manager did not correct a certain co-worker, and it drove my friend mad, since he was well known for doing his duties. Now, because of his co-worker's lack of work ethic, it reflected upon him. I am sure you have heard a story like this before. It happens every day. This, however, is an interesting case study for you, so please follow along. This friend now owns his own establishment. A short time later I met this friend again and the conversation turned to problems of the internal nature. His new mindset was very interesting. He told me that two of his employees were having work-related problems, and that he thought it was best to just let them handle it. This is very typical of people in leadership positions. They find it easier to stay out of problems than to try and solve them. They bury their head in the sand until the storm is over. With this method, the problem does not go away; it goes into hiding. It gets covered up by the morning-after syndrome—the idea that a different light or a new day "makes it all better." Sorry, I am not buying it. That is what I consider the fantasy world. Now, wake up to reality. Reality says take control. Any person who is feeling cheated, disrespected, or simply hurt needs to be heard, and it is your job as a HLT to hear them. The release of the problem creates a positive, where a negative used to live. Your job is to see the issues and treat each issue as a goal. Deal with each issue or problem as quickly as they come up. Most people quit their job, not because of what they do, but because of how they feel while doing it. The two employees I mentioned earlier, who were having a work dispute, both quit. Their boss, my friend, did not have the backbone to seek out the problem and create a way for it to go away. They quit because they expected someone to mediate their problems. They expected their leader to lead, and although he is my friend, he is no leader. He is as guilty as his previous manager. Instead of building, which is a leader's job, they let deterioration set in. People do not lead themselves; they must be taught and led. The trickle-down effect from that lack of leadership could, and does, bring many companies to their destruction. The key people leave and the work suffers. The attitudes are negative and the fire goes out. Your job as manager is to prevent problems.

I mention the prevention of problems in two different lights. One, problems are unavoidable, so it is your job to solve the issues with all parties involved by seeking the truth and not the easiest exit; and two, focus on your job from that higher place, and shine the light on the potential problems before they happen.

The little effort you put out now can solve major issues in the future, and that is the truth.

The Challenge

I challenge you today to go above your workplace and see the personnel that are not happy. See the problems in your company, and seek the real truth as to why happiness and growth are not constant.

The best way I know is to talk to your employees and customers. Listen to them and, more importantly, go to that higher place and try to understand them. The words they speak are where half the truth lies. The other half lies in you. You cannot wish that things would become better. They only become better when you have the inner strength to make them better. Anything else is fantasy. My guess is that 95 percent of problems can be solved through communication. Start tomorrow, I challenge you.

The Higher Level View

This view cannot be seen from inside your office. You must get up from your mental desk and seek out the challenge. This will be a feeling like no other, because you will have to test yourself. You have to walk the walk of the person you want to be, and rise above the person you are or were. The top is where you are. Do not look for someone else to take charge. You take charge. Wishing the problems will go away doesn't work. Problems have to be taken care of by you. A HLT knows the trickle down begins and ends with them. You must seek out the potential problems. Get your HLT team together, and fix it or prevent the problems. Then, and only then, will you have peace in your company. Anything left to chance will only hide and raise its ugly head later. See inside yourself, and wake up that person that is strong.

8. Have I shown appreciation and have I earned the respect of my employees and customers?

This is not just about raises for employees and discounts for customers. It is deeper than that.

Anyone can put a figure on a job completed. It is a numbers and percentage game. The more they make for the company, the more you can, and should, pay them. The more volume the client orders, the bigger discount you can give, if you choose. This comes from the head. In contrast, appreciation comes from the heart and soul. It is a realization that you are nothing without your employees and customers. That realization is what takes you to that higher level. It is that force that stays with you, and it is felt by both employees and customers.

Sincerity is the real magic that creates a great and comfortable workplace. Too many times, appreciation is assumed. Action speaks louder than words. Only at the dark times do the true feelings of appreciation come out. Generally, it is too late when it does. A great leader, a HLT leader shows appreciation all the time. This responsibility to show appreciation is yours. That feeling that is generated by appreciation is at the top of the trickle-down theory. When you spend time in a business, you can feel, or not feel, the appreciation towards the employees and customers. If you feel the appreciation, you will continue to patronize this establishment. I had a discussion with a friend who is in the farm implement service industry. We talked about costs and the fine line between profits for the company and fairness to the customer. I was seeking the truth which lies in the middle. He pointed out that in many cases, as long as customers get what they need, they are happy. In those cases, service is king, not necessarily the cost. I believe the equalizer in fighting this internal battle is not always one of numbers; it is one of appreciation. Quality and effort is at the forefront, but your honest appreciation will rise above cost increases. When my father was young man, working for a tire company, his boss told him to get cleaned up, because he was taking him out for a steak dinner. During the dinner, his boss told him just how much he appreciated my father's effort. I know my father, and that meant more to him than money. Appreciation is gold. Use it only if it comes from your heart.

Respect sounds a lot like appreciation, but there is a difference. I believe that respect is something that is developed over time. In most cases, you cannot feel the respect while it is being created, but it becomes apparent after the fact. The reason is that no one gives respect easily. It must be earned. I have heard many say, "I don't agree with that person, but I respect them." My late uncle taught at a Colorado University. His teaching was extremely tough. However, he was tough for a reason. While the school year was in full swing, the students were pushed, and I am sure my uncle was not their favorite teacher. In the next few years a remarkable thing happened. My uncle started to receive letters and phone calls from his past students. They told him that his class was by far their toughest. Now, as they entered the real world, they realized that they were well prepared. Most admitted that because they made it through his storm first, that test allowed them to enter their business life with confidence and to excel beyond their expectations. Their letters were ones of respect. They did not say how much they loved the guy. They talked about respect. Respect is sometimes doing the tough things when they need to be done, not taking the easiest way out, which most do. At the time it is not pleasant, however, when you look back at the experience, you realize that it was the right thing to do. After this, respect of a person becomes clear. With time, the emotions are taken out of the equation, and the right decision becomes clear. In many cases, leaders try to be liked. That usually leads to weakness and giving in to requests we know are not beneficial to the company. You know the decision would hurt that person in the long run. If you give into the wrong decision to be liked, then your employees will like you, but they will not respect you. It is like a child who wants to play on the roof. Since you let them, they like you, but you know that they could get hurt. Say no, and they will respect you, because your decision is based on the big picture. That is one side of the story.

Now as a practicing HLT, let us look at respect from the other side of the fence. Respect is a two-way street. You must also give employees the respect they deserve.

My uncle was given respect, because he was doing what was in the best interest of his students. In this case, respect also worked the other way. He respected those who took on the task, because he knew deep-down inside that it would help them excel in the real world. When both the students and my uncle saw the light, they entered the land of the HLT.

As a leader, you must rise above the easy way out. You must make the hard decisions that are beneficial to all and not waver. In return, you will earn the respect of others, although not immediately. It will take time, because our brains only deal in the present. Trust in the future and the big picture, and respect will emerge.

The Higher Level View

I am attempting to awaken the leader in you. Once you have awakened, then you will begin your self-examination. By examination, you will realize all you really need to be is a gatherer of minds, the instigator of awareness, and the engineer of action. There is a need for unselfish HLTs in the business world. However, all leadership begins with you. It is not a class you can take, not an Ivy League school you can attend. It begins with you. Selfish people are not good managers or leaders. They are so self-absorbed; they cannot let others shine in fear of being outshined. They are afraid to let others grow, because someone may outgrow them. They cannot forget about themselves long enough to focus on the customer. I see it every day in just about every business, and that is a shame. The art of management must lie in the gift of communication, and it must be used by you always.

Chapter Thirteen: The HLT Employee

"Efficiency is when the mind and the body work together for the good of the cause."

DID YOU ACTUALLY think I was going to let anyone that works for someone else or for a company off the hook? If I did, it would mean that I believe that the deterioration of American business is all management's fault. Sorry, nice try, but we (employees) are the body and soul of American business. The fact is we have gotten soft. Our work ethic is in the negative column and our own mentality has gone dormant. They (who ever they are) push for higher education in business, and our government keeps pumping money into a system that, yes, needs educators, but the fact is most education begins after school. It is called experience and the willingness to learn. I have known many people with a college education that are the worse business people I have ever met. I also have seen people with no formal education and I considered them business geniuses. The biggest attributes of these business geniuses were people skills and common sense.

I will now be addressing the majority of the human race: the employee. Society has a tendency to put all the intellectual responsibility on the owners and managers. Business mentality does trickle down and, as I mentioned earlier, it all starts with the top. However, now it is your turn to create the trickle down of great happenings; and even though you are not the boss, the intellectual trickle-down theory starts and stops with you.

Each step in a stairway must be strong or you will never go higher. It is an interesting phenomenon of how employee mentalities do not wake up until they are actually put on the spot and pressed to perform. Most employees allow their minds to be deflated by their boss and it becomes dormant. That is, in part, because you have a selfish leader, but also because you allowed it to happen.

In many cases, your thoughts and ideas will be suppressed and that is a sick reality in the business world. You must accept that fact, but never stop driving that mentally to save yourself from being mentally sheltered. The concept of the top always being where you are is very critical as an employee. You cannot change what is above you. However, you are in charge and responsible for what happens below you. I use the word above and below not as a degrading symbol but as a reality, because business society is formed that way, unfortunately. I do not like it, because it keeps thoughts in a stair step succession, which is like being mentally ranked, so to speak.

As a HLT, you must create that self-empowerment within and know that you will do your job the best that anyone can and then go beyond. I cannot promise that you will get the rewards you deserve, and most likely you will not (that depends on your leader), but that is not what a HLT is. A HLT does their job no matter what the circumstances, because self-pride is built in, they are building their own foundation. To grow as an individual and in your company, you must first impress yourself. The rest, you cannot really control.

I find that most people that do not advance in their own company or that create the trickle down of bad happenings in their company are the ones that accept things as they are. You must go above your job and seek ways to achieve your personal success which is directly tied to the success of your company. Once again, this is for you, and if your company's owner or manager is worth their salt and prove their HLT status, they will witness your effort and should reward you on that effort. The real world is this. Your manager will definitely witness your faults and errors and, unfortunately, the negatives will be magnified by one hundred. Your assets will generally go overlooked; that is a sad reality. My father-in-law was known to say, "You can do one hundred things in a row that are right and no one will notice or give you credit, but you do one thing wrong and the whole world will listen." My father always said, "If you do your job well, no matter what it is, no one will probably notice, but you will and that is where pride is born."

The greatest self-empowerment tool is mistakes. I believe they can be a negative or a positive. If you do not learn from them, they are devastating. If you do learn and never repeat them, they can be gold.

LLT do not learn. They keep repeating the same mistakes over and over again. A HLT will stack them up like a foundation to a house. They are now part of your structure and who you are and always will be.

Now let us go higher and enter the land of a HLT. If you, as a HLT, are aware that you can make mistakes, then you will be more diligent in looking for potential mistakes. On the other hand, if you are self-absorbed as a LLT is, and you believe that you cannot make a mistake, then you will. I want an employee who knows that they can make a mistake. That way they are more cautious and better able to prevent mistakes; that is powerful. A friend of mine once told me that he never will use a certain company again because they made a mistake. My question to him was, "How did the company react to the mistake?" He told me he really did not care, and that he was done with them. I will give my business to someone if they made a mistake, depending if they left me with the impression that they were going to do something about it, so that it doesn't happen again. If it is a company that does not care or show remorse then, yes, they will not get my business again. Let us now go to the real world and I will show you what I mean. This chapter is not for the employees that do their job, but for those that do not.

Entering the Real World

My wife and I visited an area clothing store to search for a new sports jacket for me. After a long search, we found a rack of jackets that we believed would work. After some careful HLT brainstorming moments as to color, actual need, and cost issues, we agreed what type of jacket would fulfill my needs. However, they did not have my size on the rack. I asked the young saleslady if these were the only jackets that they had. Her answer was that she believed that rack was all they had and that she was sorry. Another young employee overheard our conversation. She politely mentioned that she certainly could go in the back and at least make an attempt to find out if that was all they had. You guessed it. She came back with the jacket I wanted and in my size. Beaming with pride, and rightfully so, she was a HLT. The first young lady has a few miles to go before entering the land of the HLT. I do believe that she learned a lesson by the second lady taking charge and solving our issue. She can become an HLT, if she learned from that lesson. I do not put all the blame on the young lady. It may be her first working experience outside the house and we have all been there. I blame two people for her lack of thinking: her manager for not telling her all the possibilities of business that can come up in her position and giving her the tools to solve those potential issues, and I blame her parents for not teaching their child business principles and how she fits in with that formula. My guess is that the manager assumed that she would naturally know what to do and the parent assumed the manager would tell her. Why should the parent do it? They were just happy to see her working, not learning.

Sorry for the truth, but there it is. They both were cop-outs and both were LLTs for not going the extra mile and teaching her. The second lady demonstrated what builds HLT dreams and businesses. She went to that next and higher level and insured that we would come back, when—after the experience with the first salesperson—we most likely would have not have. We left that store saddened and feeling good all at the same time. We were disappointed that the first young lady stopped at greatness, or at the least just doing her job, but excited that the second young lady created a great trickle-down effect which is an HLT trademark. The second salesperson used awareness and focus out of her personal toolbox. She created a personal awareness of the customer's needs and then focused on the solution. She won, the company won and the customer won—another HLT trademark. This example can be attributed to every aspect of business and life. It is that simple. Life and business are that simple.

This next example is more about personal responsibility than an actual event. My mind is confused in trying to understand why employees do not sound the alarm when they see a customer issue. It certainly is in part, I believe, because there is no system set up for manager and employee interaction. This goes back to what I mentioned earlier about the employee knowing more about the actual business than the ones running it in most cases. Not as much as the big picture that a manager must look at, but more so the nuts and bolts of the business. Employees are the ones that see the issues that are created in the business itself and are the ones that more often deal with the actual customer. They are the eyes and ears of the customer and should be the voice also, but generally are left out of major decisions when it comes to the operations of the company.

However, this chapter is about you—the employee—and you are at the top of the trickle-down theory. Remember the business theory chapter? The example where the server almost ran into the patrons at the buffet at the blind corner? When I asked a server if that situation was awkward, she said, "Yes," but made no attempt to solve the problem. I certainly can pick this situation apart and once again go back to the manager's responsibility, but it is also the employee's responsibility to take the issue and turn it into action and then to the solution. In some business formats you are unable to because of your restrictions as not being the boss. However, your mentality as an HLT should be to create the awareness of the problems and situations of your customer and do "your job" and react. Then it is up to the manager to handle the problem or prevent the problems from occurring in the future.

As employees, we tend to pass the buck when it comes to responsibility. Most say, "Go see the manager." When, in fact, you should have already trained yourself for any situation. A HLT knows where the top is in their world—they are at the top. In our example, the employee has seen near misses and probably accidents with the patrons and servers. An HLT would have addressed the issue with a problem-solving meeting with his or her fellow employees and brought this matter up to the manager, recorded the date and their effort to solve this matter, and let the chips fall where they may, all the while knowing that they did their part. It was now up to the powers to be to implement the solution. A LLT would have turned a blind eye and allowed this circus to continue and, by doing so, increased the odds of someone getting hurt or, at the least, shaken up. Afterward, they would have said, "Someone should have done something to resolve that!"

A HLT employee is the one that must stand up and change life for the better and do their part to prevent all bad situations from happening, even though others will not.

When I brought this situation up to a friend of mine he said, "That is why they carry insurance." My friend is not a HLT. I did not work at that restaurant and really had no stake in that situation, but I changed it, because that is who I am. Who do you want to be—a talker (LLT) or a doer (HLT)? Think about that.

This last situation plays on both of the last two examples and says a lot about the importance of your position in your company. In fact, the least paying and the least noticeable positions in terms of clout, pay, and social status are usually the most important.

Another friend of mine and I were having a conversation about banking. He was a banker and a member of the board of directors at a local bank. He said that in his opinion, the most important people in a bank were the tellers. Now I in no way want to downplay the importance of loan officers in the bank, and I am sure I will ruffle some of my friends feathers in the banking business, but what my friend said made a lot of sense to me. The officers and their networking and their innovative ways of bringing in customers and their financial intelligence in making their way through the complicated financial world of buying, selling etc. is what brings in the customers, but after the smoke settles and you have obtained your customer, who dictates if they will stay? Most likely it is the tellers and the people in the front lines of your business. If the loan officer does not care about me, then they will not get my business to start with. If the business is transacted, then all I will see from there on will be the tellers where I make my deposits, withdraws, and payments; and they had better treat me with respect and be friendly or I will lose that feeling of loyalty with that bank. I can speak from experience, because I have done it. I have moved variable amounts of money to different banks because I lost that feeling. It was not a lot of money, but it was real money, and it was their money to use.

Now, I have just shown you that your job, no matter what your position is, can be as important, if not more important, than your manager's. Do your job right and you will get the positive response from your customers, and they will respond to your boss and that will give you the boost that you need for your career. Not only do it for the customer, but do it because it is what HLTs do. You need to believe in your HLT mind that those customers are coming in because of you. You do everything in "your" power to bring them in. Keep them thinking that there isn't another business on earth that does what you do and can do it as well as you can. That is an HLT employee.

The Challenge

I challenge you to go beyond your normal thinking and strive to take care of every possible need and want for the customer that you are servicing. If you are not directly tied to a customer then go beyond what you get paid to do. That is what an HLT does and is. Think of ways to improve on your job and or do it with more efficiency. I challenge you to be the one who sounds the alarm if there are errors or if the path of satisfying a customer is being interrupted. Be the one who waves the flag that there is a better way to do things that makes everyone happy and content. I also challenge you to become the reason that your company is successful, not the reason it is in turmoil. Be the one that the customer asks for and be the reason the customer wants to even come into your business in the first place. I challenge you to become the best employee that the company has ever seen and, by that act alone, you will most likely move up to be the best manager that company has ever had. Now that is self-empowerment.

The Higher Level View

HLTs are the company, your actions are the company, and your thoughts are the company. Your desire as a HLT is to make your company the best it can be. You will start the trickle down of great happenings by opening up your unselfish toolbox and working with others everyday to create the best service for your customers and do the best job for your employer. You, as an HLT, will inspire others and teach them how to be HLTs and great employees. If you are a managing employee, it is your responsibility to acquire experience and intelligence and pass it down, and that will elevate you further up the corporate ladder. More importantly, it will give you self-worth and self-accomplishment. Your job as a HLT employee is to look within yourself and go above your job and your business and ask what you can do better than you did yesterday for your employer. Ask what you can do for your customer that was better than you did the day before and, by that thought alone, you will rise up to that next level.

Chapter Fourteen: The HLT on Personal Finance

"Financial intelligence is not about money. It is about the mentality of money."

AS I STARTED this chapter, I actually felt like personal finance should be so soaked in common sense. So much so, that it didn't need explained. I certainly am not going to waste a lot of time on the nuts and bolts of personal finance, because it has been repeated on radio and television shows for years and, apparently, no one is listening. I am, however, going to focus on the forces that are positive and negative in relationship to personal finance. The answer to personal finance does not begin with these wonderful financial teachers. It begins and ends with your personal mentality. It is now time to prevent these negatives in your financial life before they happen, not after. Personal finance is really just a number's game. It should be that simple, if your mind is clear. However, ego, emotions, and pride make the mind extremely cloudy. The trickle-down theory was created by a HLT. HLTs believe that it really doesn't matter what you make financially, it is about how you cover yourself on the downside of your financial decisions. By managing risk, you have stopped the trickle down of bad happenings. This formula is extremely simple. First, you must build your unwavering self-empowered foundation. The words chiseled in the base of that foundation should read, "Can I afford to do this if the worst would happen to me?" If the answer is no, then your decision is no. If yes, then obviously it would be yes. That is not what happens, is it? Most of you will take a few moments to make your decision, but I will bet that you will come up with more reasons why you should buy an item than why you should not. I am right, am I not? So now, in my quest for answers as to why everyone struggles with personal finances and why debt has become so common place, I raised my mentality, and here is my personal opinion on that subject. It happens when we let the ego and pride in all of us win the empowerment battle. Self-empowerment is common sense. A LLT gives into the ego and pride. LLTs believe you are what you drive. If you drive a nice car, then you are successful. If you own a big house, then you are wealthy. In fact, that may be as far from the truth as it can be.

When the mentality of others dictate and change your common sense foundation, you no longer have self-empowerment. More importantly, when you do not listen to your own voice of common sense, then you also have lost your self-empowerment. It is as simple as that. If the little person "on your left shoulder" convinces you that you need to buy this item because you deserve it or others expect it, and you disregard the big person "on your right shoulder," then you are the king of the LLTs.

Do you honestly believe because you have a good job now that you will always have a good job? Do you believe that because you are healthy now that you will never get sick or be in an accident—both which would change your life and your income? If those are truly what you believe, then you are opening yourself up to potential financial destruction. That was meant to wake you up, and I hope it worked. You must take control of your financial life and quit walking through this world blind, if you are going to be a HLT. You must decide if you are going to build your foundational life on the edge of a cliff or build your foundation on solid ground. It is as simple as dropping the pride and living your life with a slow moving powerful force that always moves forward, but is smart enough to cover what they have built behind them. There is one thought that you need to remember as we enter into the world of personal financial reality. Class, internal strength, integrity, honesty and honor make a HLT, not the car you drive nor the house you live in. Our mentality is getting clouded by who we all want to be instead of who we actually are.

A HLT does not have anything to prove to anyone. My grandfather always said, "If you do not like the way I look, then look the other way." I remembered this from when I was young, and I believe he left it up to me to decide what that meant. I believe what he meant was, if you are going to judge me, maybe you should check your facts first about me. Maybe what I am doing with my life and my finances are more powerful and make more sense than what you are doing. I will not join you in your quest for destruction or negative attitudes or reckless financial responsibility. Apparently, you will not join me in my quest for building a positive attitude and financial intelligence. Therefore, maybe you should turn your attention in another direction. I was trying to be more diplomatic than my grandfather was and more politically correct. So, how did I do? I used this as a lead into the first real world scenario, because I do believe my grandfather was right.

However, please understand that it is not about degrading the wealthy. I could not be more pleased if a family is financially successful, because now I do not have to worry about them. It is the mentality that radiates throughout our country that you must have material items and show them off if you are to be considered someone. That mentality certainly will destroy your mental being, not to mention your wallet. To be someone, financially speaking, you just need to use common sense in every financial decision you make.

HLT has nothing to do with wealth, but intelligence and unselfishness. The simplicity of financial intelligence is about proportions which in a sense is a number's game. If you make a million dollars a year, a portion should be saved for future security for your family, housing, entertainment, etc. If you make twenty thousand dollars a year, the same principle applies. Simple financial thinking means you do not spend everything you earn. A higher level yet is, if you do not have it, accept that, and live your life with that current thought process. Find your self-empowerment in that mental reality, not in false fantasy. I have witnessed people who have made or inherited a huge amount of money and ended up broke. It challenges your mind as to how they could go through that much money. I have also witnessed people who made less than forty-thousand dollars a year and became rich. It is all about the mentality of a proportionate thought process. Keeping it simple is gold. Living within your means is translated into covering any worst-case scenario that can happen in your life and structuring your life to live within the guidelines of your income. By that thought alone, you have stopped the trickle down of bad happenings in your financial life. The financial experts all say that you should have an emergency fund. I call that the nuts and bolts of personal finance, and I do agree. However, you should live every day with that mindset. That mindset simply being: Preserve what you have, and build from there. That will keep these little financial hiccups from turning into a big mountain of financial burdens.

"You do not need to live in a castle to mentally walk with kings and queens."

Entering the Real World

I am staying in the mentality aspect of personal finance in my examples, because the powerful mind, not your pocket book, will determine your wealth and your security.

What is the intent of a vehicle? To get to your destination, right? What is the intent of a house? Shelter, right? You must begin with that mental thought process first, and grow proportionately from that point. Those who do are the ones who become secure, if not wealthy. I am not degrading or judging the people who have a big truck or a large home. I think it is absolutely wonderful, as long as two mental thought processes are present. First, that they are secure enough and can afford the payments of that house or vehicle, if the worst case situation would happen in their financial life; and second, that they do not look down upon others who do not drive the same nice vehicle as they do. They may actually be a LLT for driving the big truck, and for thinking that way in the first place.

This first example is one that certainly can rub a few people wrong, but that is not my intent. It is simply to make my point and to challenge and strengthen your personal financial spirit. I can pick many situations where this mentality plays out in my hometown. A gentleman drives down the road in a very used vehicle. He is passed and looked at and judged by this particular lady in a very large expensive vehicle. Now, I would be very happy if her proportionate financial life and financial obligations are under control. The only problem I have is that I know all about her. I know that her family lives paycheck to paycheck. I know their status in our community. I know her family's mentality, and I know her family members are candidates for LLTs.

I am not assuming I know the truth. That is why I make the bold statement that they have no self-empowerment. Their financial mentality is based on society and status and not on financial intelligence. Now, let us break down each party in this picture. The driver of the large vehicle will automatically look down on the driver in the old vehicle, and put herself in a place which is a false fairy tale. She has no self-empowerment, because she lives in the fantasy world, and because of her own self-absorbed mental peer pressure. She will wake up to reality if anything negative should happen in her world. She does not have a solid foundation. It is built on lies and the assumption that she is financially strong. Another factual issue with her is that the interest paid on her car loan for five years opens the window to her mental financial instability. The fact that she doesn't even need this big vehicle tells me she just doesn't use common HLT sense. This mentality is the root of all evil for our personal finance. It leads to credit card debt, which has been blown way out of proportion for the everyday household. It starts with owning property for status, not necessity.

Now, let us visit the HLT that was driving the old used vehicle and was being looked down upon. This particular gentleman was driving an old vehicle that is missing a little paint and makes a few noises and blows a little smoke, but does its job and gets him to work every day. This is a job where he earns a decent living. By driving this old truck, he can deposit half his paycheck into the bank every month. Now, here is the rest of the story. This particular gentleman also has a three-year old used truck in the garage at home. Its costs half the price of the vehicle the lady was driving and looks just as nice. Did I mention is paid for? It has half the miles the lady had on hers, because the HLT decides to keep the miles off the new truck and drive the old one around town and use common sense instead of giving into societies peer pressure, even though he takes ribbing by driving this old truck. The HLT very clearly sees the numbers and the common sense that is in front of him and is not clouded by what a lower mentality will think of him. His money goes into the bank in his family's account and not to the banks' pockets. He will use the money saved for his family's financial foundation and security, and will not give into societies' false mentality.

So in essence, she was looking down upon him; but in the higher mental world, he was looking down (but not judging) her. A LLT will say, when seeing an expensive vehicle going down the road, "I wished I had that." A HLT will say, "I am glad I do not have their payments." It is all how you look at it.

Look at finances through a higher common sense place, not through a lower fantasy mind. Be aware. When you use common sense in finances, the majority of the people in your life (who are broke by the way) will probably ridicule you. If you stay true to your convictions and do not waver from what is right, you will build another strong layer to your self-empowerment which is your foundation. A HLT is a leader. A HLT is only a follower when the ship is going the right way.

The second example would be the second step in financial self-empowerment, and that would be to self-empower others. HLTs are leaders and teachers. Once you have become financially strong, you need to learn to change minds so that strong self-financial empowerment can reproduce. It certainly has been the teachings of financial responsibility that has been handed down to me from generation to generation.

Unfortunately, from what I witness, mine may be the last generation of financial intelligence. Credit card amounts have escalated out of control and that happened when prosperity was abundant in our land. The wants have changed our mental thought process and superseded our needs. Worse yet, that mentality is being passed down to our children. The example that my parents set—of taking care of your needs and your family's needs first then if there is anything left, use it for wants—is now gone. Poor examples are being set today. Our value system will likely be gone forever. The only thing that has gotten our nation through its hard times in the past was Americans using common sense, and that mentality is fading fast.

Specifically, I am targeting the parents. The word "no" was a common word used by my parents when the wants of a young boy became apparent. They said no to teach me values, and the difference between wants and needs was hard work. You had to work, save, and only then should the item become yours. Today, parents have gotten soft. They feel like they have to buy their children everything they want. The first whimper from the child, and the parents cave in. The values that were passed down to us, and made us financially, intelligent are gone. The LLT parent doesn't understand that their children's disappointment is only temporary, but giving in will have long-term effects. Their child forgets about that want in a very short time. When they get older, they will not even remember the item they were crying about.

What is built by the word "no" is a deep-seeded system called values. Giving into their every want will destroy their future and their drive to earn what they want. The reason I bring this up is because to say "no" is to not only build up the values of your child, but to also build up your self-empowerment as a parent. When this empowerment is established, the financial foundation is built. You can begin to build financial mountains from here. This will include saving money for your child to go to college, your own retirement, and an easy feeling as you go through life. These are more important than money, and this will become apparent, because you will not worry about money. The only difference between this example and the previous one is that in the first, you have to grow up and say "no" to yourself. In this example, you have to grow up and say "no" to someone else. Both take self-empowerment and an inner strength to achieve.

Now, are you wondering when you get to live life? Well, that really doesn't matter too much, because you are now a HLT, and HLTs are unselfish. If you show discipline and say no to yourself in the short term, you will reap the long-term rewards. Your life starts when this behavior gives you a peaceful feeling, and a peaceful feeling is what living is all about. If something happened to you, and you do not get to reap the rewards of your patience, your family will benefit from your unselfishness. This is the giving spirit that a HLT possesses. So, either way, you win. By creating and living with these values, and teaching your child these values, you are giving them their future.

Take time to include your child in your finances and sacrifice you are making, so that they can have a good life. Tell them what you want, but explain how you decided to hold off so you could take care of what you needed first. Give them examples. Now create their world, and teach them about the sacrifices they can make. Show them what their reward will be if they help you with the family finances. These days are golden. If you miss this opportunity, you have kept your child in the circle of debt forever, and it is your fault. Do not make excuses, make memories. The ability to create self-empowerment is certainly key. That mindset is needed to hold your ground. Be committed to doing the right thing and seeking the financial truth. This is half the battle. You need to slow down and make secure financial decisions.

I am absolutely blown away by seemingly intelligent people making less than intelligent decisions or making decisions without any thought process altogether.

First, they make decisions too quickly without looking at the long-term effects. Second, they live in the fantasy world and disregard what they actually can afford. Along with that, they do not plan for the unknown. Only if you are lucky will you avoid financial pitfalls of life.

A friend of mine complained that at every Christmas his family comes in and he barely has enough room for all of them to sleep. He said he is contemplating buying a bigger house to solve that issue. I asked him if he liked his house. He said yes. I asked him if he liked the neighborhood. He said yes. I asked him if it was otherwise big enough for his everyday life. He said yes. To upgrade to a bigger house he would have to invest approximately another thirty-thousand dollars, not to mention the hassle of moving and leaving a very nice, friendly neighborhood. At the age of eighty years young, that sounds like a hassle to me.

I suggested that he put up half his guests at the local motel for two days. This would run him about three-hundred dollars and his problem would be solved. It is just for sleeping, anyway. He said he hadn't thought about that. He now does it, and everyone is happy. Normally, you would think that this is not a good financial plan, because he has to pay three-hundred dollars. However, it certainly beats thirty-thousand plus interest, plus extra taxes, heating bills, and miscellaneous other expenses just two days a year.

He had focused on the house being too small. Instead, he should have gone to a higher place and viewed the whole picture, which was the guest accommodations, not his small house.

By doing this, he could have solved his financial situation or, better yet, kept a future financial problem from occurring. He looked at his problem from inside instead of from above the problem.

Why was this solution not discovered? I believe he did not open the toolbox and use the handy tool called focus. The answer was right there all the time if he was looking for it.

The next example is of another friend of mine that was going to buy a rental house. After asking my opinion, I asked him a few questions. From his answers, I knew I could attempt to give him an intelligent answer. My first question was, "What is your cash flow above and beyond your bank payment, taxes, and insurance." He thought it would be about a break-even situation. Right there I stopped him and told him he was not in the mental and financial position to be in real estate.

He asked why, and I simply told him that he failed to cover the downside of his financial venture. After he told me of his fantasy plan and his perfect world in real estate, I proceeded to give him a multitude of probable situations that would burst his fantasy bubble. It did burst his bubble and, thank goodness, he did not go through with the deal. HLT is about covering the worst-case scenarios. The LLT gets lost in the roses and forgets about the thorns. They actually talk themselves into the positive aspects of the deal and mentally refuse to look at the negatives.

Self-empowerment is when you have control over the negatives and the positives. Until you have all the potential problems solved, you have left your venture to fate. In most cases, that will drag your personal finances and your future into a life of despair.

If my friend could not find a deal where he has a positive cash flow that covered no renter, damage, increased taxes, insurance, and attorney fees to remove renters when they do not pay, he should not do the deal. If he did, he certainly should keep his day job, because he would need it to pay for his poor judgment.

The last example is another mentality which disturbs our personal finance issues. There is a television program that comes on every night in which a buyer is searching for that perfect home. In this show, the family has several choices with various prices. The mentality that exists in this show is, in my opinion, what has created the housing boom and, incidentally, the housing bust.

A LLT believes that the candy is worth the risk and, generally, they go for the candy and disregard the risk. Then they pay more than the house is actually worth. In most cases, they choose the house that costs more, even though they admit it was at the top or over their budget.

Then, to add insult to injury, they do some remodeling after the purchase. Each buyer has done their part to drive up the market and create the real estate bubble that has emerged. This bubble was created by LLTs who believe that their home is an investment. Instead, it should be looked at as a home.

A HLT looks at their home as a place for shelter, warmth, safety, and function, not as a status symbol. You spend at least twice for a house than it is worth just by financing. Then you put your family at risk if you lose your income or make a bad loan choice. You become house poor and no longer can do the things you would really like to do because of your house debt. So then you turn to credit cards to do those things which compound the issue. Now you can't even reap the rewards of the money that you have put into your house until you sell it. All this because of the almighty status symbol. When the fact is very few people even know where you live. I repeat again, the only one you need to impress is you. A HLT is impressed by their own financial intelligence, not by making bad choices based off of social pressures.

The Challenge

I challenge you to stand tall today and make the changes that are affecting your financial life. I challenge you to get rid of those toys that cost your son that college opportunity. I challenge you to look deep inside yourself and drop that pride and ego, and discover what is more important to your life. Is it your financial future or what the other people think? I challenge you to say no and stop this spoiling mentality we have as parents, and start teaching your child financial responsibility. Start leading by example, and do a little growing up yourself. I also challenge you to quit talking a good game, and open your mind to find the solutions to all your financial problems. Search for the truth and the best possible solution. I challenge you to open your mind to all who might have a solution to your problem, because the reality is you do not know it all. And I challenge you to explore all the down sides if the worst were to happen. By that act alone you have controlled your destiny or at least increased your odds of success.

The Higher Level View

The power of the mind is so enormous that if let loose without structure, it can destroy. With discipline and common sense, it can build. Look at it like the strongest bull. If you let it roam with reckless abandon, it will destroy crops, structures, and life. However, if the power is harnessed, it can plow the furrows for crops to grow, lift the walls for a strong foundation, and create a life that has peace and strength.

Money does not solve financial issues, intelligence does. You must now go to that higher level, and create your own foundation. To put it simply, the people you are trying to impress will not help you with your payments. I promise you that. It will have to come from you and your resources. Your strength and your inner power will create your foundation. By living below your means, you can become bigger than your finances. Instead of the storm taking over you, you will be the sunshine that will be over the storm. The clouds and the storms are an earthly event. The spirit of the mind is bigger and higher than it is. Do not get caught up in the pride and ego that consumes the earth. Go to the higher heavens for your answer to financial intelligence. By thinking at a higher level and using common sense in every financial detail, and by not getting consumed by the artificial pressures of mankind, you will begin to create a powerful, but peaceful force in your financial life and the trickle down will begin to happen. The self-empowerment and self control will radiate from you and will be passed down to the next generation, and you will have done your job on this earth.

Chapter Fifteen: The HLT on Driving Mentality

"No amount of time saved and no amount of mental effort given will equal a life taken."

IN MY OPINION, there is no other aspect of our lives that shows our true colors and our intelligence as a person than the way we drive. Go to that higher place with me for a moment. Does your driving reflect your personality, your risk factor, and your awareness of others? Does it reflect your selfishness or unselfishness as a person? The constant goal of a HLT is to get to your destination safely, and to help others arrive at their destination safely. By all means, do not be the one that creates a trickle down of bad happenings. Accidents and death will occur, that is a fact of life. However, how many lives could be saved if we all used unselfishness and HLT in our thought process while driving? Earlier, I told you how many people lost their lives while driving. This chapter is about saving your life and the life of others. It is just plain old respect.

The most powerful thought you can have when driving is ask yourself, "Do I want to hurt or kill someone else or myself?" Yes or no? This is not a question with a maybe. It is a question with a yes or no answer. If your answer is that you do not care, then I will pray for you and your selfish self being. If you believe this is an absurd question, then you are now thinking at a higher level. Welcome aboard. If you ask one hundred people if their intent is to hurt or kill someone while they are driving, one hundred of them will say, "Of course not." However, their actions demonstrate something different. If you take the question too lightly or you do not think at all times, then you contradict your intent.

Let me discuss some poor mentalities of driving. Speeding, for example. Isn't the law clear enough about the speed you are supposed drive? There is a well-presented sign reminding you every so often what the speed is. Those who speed are saying they are bigger than the law. A HLT understands that the speed limit is there for safety. Obey the law of safety. Sounds like common sense to me, doesn't it to you?

Let's take another example. Take a simple stop sign. Anyone unclear about what this sign actually means? Your lazy mentality is showing if you do not stop as the law requires, and HLTs are not lazy. How about passing? If done recklessly to save a few minutes of time, it can possibly take your life or the life of another human being.

Does this act show your level of thinking? It sure does. Taking unnecessary risks shows immaturity and lack of intelligence. In other words, a LLT mentality. Erring on the side of caution shows strength, intelligence, and unselfishness, a HLT mentality.

After driving home one day, we nearly had a head-on collision with another vehicle driven by a person who just had to save a precious few seconds. That greedy thought could very well have cost my wife and me our lives. His few seconds were more important than our lives. Seconds can save or cost a life. That driver was a classic LLT. Only because I had my awareness tool activated, was I able to slow down, and pull over to avoid the accident, sparing our lives and his. I wonder if he appreciated my effort or recognized that I may have saved his life. I doubt it.

Control is a word some people do not like to use. This is true when it comes to controlling people. I am using the word in the sense of controlling situations and not letting bad win. That day I did take control of the bad action taken by someone else, and I made everything all right. That is why I strive everyday to become a HLT. It makes things better.

I knew a man I respected for his business mind. However, when I drove with him to one of his business meetings, he displayed the most LLT adolescent behavior I have ever witnessed from an adult. He was rude and took a lot of unnecessary chances with our lives and with the lives of other drivers. He tailgated when there was nowhere for the other driver to go, even if they did speed up. Even if he did get around them, they met us at the next stop light. He actually thought that because he was late for his meeting (because he did not leave early enough), everyone should get out of his selfish way. I never looked at him with respect again.

There are no part-time HLTs. He was good at business, but dropped the ball on driving. He was the driver you looked at and wondered, "What is that guy thinking?" Driving tests you every minute of your drive. It tests you, because most everyone around you will not follow the rules. Your test is to do your job as a HLT, and not join the pack like a LLT. It is very tough to not go with the flow and follow others. For example, if ten cars go by you ten miles over the speed limit, does that make it okay for you to go ten miles over the limit? No, it does not, and a HLT knows that. If you are going the speed limit and someone pushes up behind you, whether they pass you or not, you are the leader and they are the follower. You are obeying the law; they are not. Never forget that, ever.

If you do what is right and stick to that principle, and they get to their destination before you, you have won a victory called honor and truth. You were the leader, even though they were faster. They will always be the follower. That was the first test.

The second test is to see if you are strong enough and smart enough to attempt to control the road for all who are on the road. If someone doesn't do their job, are you alert and aware enough to make the adjustments for their mistakes to keep everyone safe? I had written this chapter right before my close encounter with a LLT. I only had one chance and, because I was aware, I changed the outcome from bad to good. I focused on getting us to our destination safely, and I avoided an accident. A HLT won and lived! The LLT lost and, on that day, I did not make my mama cry.

Being a HLT is all about self-empowerment. It is about your ability to change the outcome of a situation. By doing your job right, you avoid fifty percent of the things that can happen to you. I know I cannot change people from being selfish. I am hoping, however, that the few of us that are not selfish can save lives of those that are. Let me give you some real life examples and, hopefully open your eyes to the difference that a LLT or a HLT can make in your driving world and in your life.

Entering the Real World

Two drivers arrive at an unmarked intersection at the same time. Who has the right-of-way? Not so fast with your answer. According to the driving manual, the person on the right has the right of way. Now that mentality would be in the thinking level of an ALT. It is thinking by the book. Is that what you think? Is standard ALT thinking sufficient? No. A HLT's answer is that no one has the right-of-way.

HLTs believe that common sense takes seniority over human law, because not all humans go by the law. Therefore, common sense has to rule. If we assume that a person on the left will stop, because it is the law, you will be wrong. Those who have left this world due to that assumption would agree with me. Unfortunately, they died carrying that assumption with them. Drivers are not always going to play by the rules. We must use our actions, controlled by our higher mentality, to avoid or prevent bad happenings from occurring. If both drivers were HLTs, both would have slowed down, used caution, proceeded respectfully, and moved forward safely. Let me ask you parents, do you want your teenager going through that intersection by the book or by the HLT's law which screams common sense. By the way, parent, which law do you follow?

Do you assume that just because someone has their blinker on that they are going to turn? What if you are wrong one time? Do you assume that everyone is going to stop at a stop sign? I have noticed that only about twenty percent of people actually stop at a stop sign. A HLT will reverse the assumption and assume that no one will stop at a stop sign. According to that mental thought process, they will be ready for it.

You can control the road, if you assume the worse. If you drive mentally blind, assuming that everyone will do their job or obey the rules, then you will be let down. Good luck with that, because you will now be counting on luck and that is not what a HLT does.

While traveling down Interstate-70, my wife and I encountered a possible life-changing situation. We were following a semi-tractor trailer going around a vehicle in the right lane that was not going the speed limit. Unfortunately, this was in an area with an on ramp to the interstate. As the semi passed the car, and attempted to get back in the right lane, he encountered a car coming up the on ramp. Meanwhile, my wife and I were in the process of passing the semi truck. This was a situation where all the stars line up to shine on the bad happenings that are about to occur. Not on my watch, though. I noticed that the semi-trailer truck was not aware of the oncoming car coming up the on ramp. Since I was aware of my surroundings and knew no one was behind me, I slowed way down, just in time. The semi-truck swerved to the left to avoid hitting the car. If I had not been paying attention, I would have gotten run over by the semi-truck. I took control of the situation when others lost control.

If you are a HLT, put that into your memory banks and use it every time you get behind the wheel. The LLT might have been talking on a cell phone, daydreaming, or lost in music. A LLT probably would have been involved in an accident and could have died. It happens every day, many times a day all over the world. I am proud to say this HLT was aware of the dangers, assumed others were not, and took action to avoid disaster. If you think I am bragging, you are right. I work hard at it. Life happens that quickly. You had better be ready for it. Wake up looking for it.

One of the defining traits of a HLT is that they are very unselfish. This certainly does not change when they are behind the wheel of a vehicle. They do their job to make the road safe for all. This is HLT gold.

Another example is when a HLT is driving down a two-lane road towards evening. She notices a large piece of wood that has fallen off the back of a truck driven by a LLT who didn't make sure the wood was secure. She makes sure the traffic is clear, pulls over, and throws the wood off to the side of the road. This unselfish act is what is built inside of a HLT. It is who they are.

A LLT is driving down the same road, same piece of wood. The thought of that wood being unsafe to others does not even cross her mind. If it did, she figures that her twenty seconds is too valuable to stop and do the right thing. She goes around the wood, and continues down the road. She is grateful she saw it in time, so she did not hit it with her car. Later that night, a young lady is driving home with her young child, gets distracted for just a second, looks up sees the obstacle in the road, swerves to miss it, loses control of her car, and goes off the road. You fill in the blanks. Would this tragic scenario have played out that way if the LLT had stopped and moved the wood? Probably not. Most likely life would have gone on peacefully. However, what if those stars lined up to create bad happenings and the next day life had changed for their family? Are you going to be the one that could have saved those lives but did nothing?

I have often analyzed the mentality of those who fail to turn on their lights in the fog, because they could see fine. Did they think about the fact that maybe no one could see them? They only think of themselves and it could cause everyone hardship.

One more issue I need to get off my chest. There is a situation in my hometown where there is a highway running through a four-lane road. Each person traveling from either direction must stop before crossing the highway. I travel this particular road at least four times a day. I am quite observant on the selfish mentality that takes place at this stop sign. I approach the stop sign, stop, and wait until the coast is clear to cross the highway. In my estimation, at least eighty percent of the cars that pull up in the next lane block my view to the highway—without one regard to the fact that I am waiting and looking for vehicles speeding down the highway. It is quite apparent that not one of these drivers is thinking about others. I was there first. Respect should have been given to me, as I would have given it to them. Is your life more precious than mine? You might think so, but my mama doesn't. A LLT mentality is obvious in this example. The HLT would have stopped before blocking my view. Let me make my choice as to when it was safe to cross, and then move up and take their turn. In doing so, no one should ever get hurt at that highway crossing.

It so happens that there have been a number of accidents at that crossing, and I believe two people have died so far! Who is next? The LLT or the HLT? I pray no one. I fear many, and I am taking action to get it changed. Wish me luck fellow HLTs.

On a lighter side of driving, is the respect factor. It should also be a common sense tool, but I believe I have already shot down that theory. It is just not happening. People are too self absorbed to show respect. Let me cover this lighter side of driving with a few respect questions to stimulate that brain of yours. First, do you stop before getting to an intersection if you see a semi-tractor truck needing to make a wide turn into your lane? You don't know what I am talking about, do you? I have never seen anyone do it. What a shame. It is our job to help everyone on the road. If you keep your eyes open and your selfish nature in the trunk, you will be that unselfish person you can be proud of. Second, do you use caution when you see an out-of-state tag in front of you? Got you again, didn't I? Have you have ever been out of town, going down the highway, and either weren't sure of where your exit was or which lane to be in, or you simply missed your turn. If you say no, most likely you are still living in the land of pride and not reality. If you ever have, then don't you think others have, too? If you are following an out-of-state tag, doesn't caution come to mind since they very well may make a quick turn or suddenly slow down? Awareness of that possibility is what a HLT driver does.

Another twist to driving and part of your toolbox is pre-thought. Do you look at the radar before leaving the house on a trip? You would be surprised at the amount of people who do not. With the latest technology there is no excuse for not at least having an idea of the weather pattern you will be driving into. I have seen people run right into ice storms, hail storms, and snow storms that stopped their travel for two days, because they did not leave a day earlier or did not research the possible weather issues.

Our flight landed back in Kansas one winter day. The first thing I did as we were waiting on our luggage was to call the office and have the secretary check the radar, because I had already checked the forecast from my previous city and knew of a possible ice storm. She informed me where the ice storm was, which direction it was coming from, and I used that information to drive around the storm without incident. If I did not check on the weather pattern, we would have driven right in its icy path.

In each one of these cases a LLT could have caused issues that could have been avoided. Instead, he or she could have helped the truck driver, for example, by stopping short and letting them make their wide turn I know they appreciate that, because they have indicated that to me through their friendly gestures. This shows respect for my unselfish thought process; everyone wins. With thoughtfulness from a HLT driver, a possible accident could be avoided by an out-of-town driver unsure of directions; and a driver could have avoided being stranded in a ditch, causing the trickle-down effect to other people. Fortunately, in each case, a HLT took control of every situation and gave them a peaceful and safe outcome.

"Don't you feel silly when you pass someone, and they end up at the stop light directly behind you?"

The Challenge

I now challenge all drivers to take control of every situation that concerns you in your world of driving. It is your job as a HLT to prevent the problems, and not be the problem. I challenge you to obey all the laws, including the law of common sense. Speed limits, passing, and even that complicated-to-understand sign that says stop! I challenge you to slow down when there is an issue on the road and not speed up. I challenge you to not assume anything unless you are assuming the worst. I challenge you to seek out and beware of the irresponsible drivers and adjust your driving, so that even if they are LLTs, they will not disrupt your goal of arriving safely. I challenge you to be respectful to all who enter your world, and help other drivers reach their destinations. I challenge you to use common sense when driving in the fog, when following an out-of-state tag, and in pre-thinking your trip to avoid terrible situations. This is your job if you are a HLT. I challenge you to remember that the road is built for all, and not just you. My time is just as valuable as yours, and my life is equally as important as yours. So, please, go above the road and your world, and trade safety for time. Think about that—a HLT does.

"Leaving early can save your life or the life of others."

The Higher Level View

Two more questions before I move on. First, do you know of someone who died in an automobile accident? Second, would you trade a few minutes of your time to have them back? That is usually how much time you save when you pass someone while risking lives in the process. If you dismiss those questions with the thought that it cannot and will not happen to you or the ones you love, then you will never be a HLT. If you are to achieve HLT status, you must do your own self-examination and promise yourself that before you get in your car and take that trip that you will not take a risk on the highway, no matter what your time situation is. Always err on the side of caution. Prepare your mind and you will make smart choices. Disregard my warnings, and you have increased your odds of a disaster, which leads to regrets.

Being a HLT means you have committed yourself to being unselfish and accepting the responsibility of controlling the road, so all will be safe. There will be no rewards or praise. You will be just doing your job, because that is what HLTs do. The HLT law is the law of common sense and supersedes all other laws. I know people will not do their job on the road. I know they will make careless, reckless decisions that will harm people. However, if you do your HLT job and think and teach others to think, we can make the road a safer place. If my words and teachings save one life, then all my efforts are worth it. Contrary to what anyone says, we can save tens of thousands of lives with just a higher thinking and unselfish mentality in driving. Go to that place with me, and help me save a life. Remember, being a little late is better than not getting there at all.

By the way, on average, 41,000 people do not get to their destination every year. That is reality. Think about that the next time you start your car.

Chapter Sixteen: The HLT on Political Mentality

IT WAS SUGGESTED to me not to write about the glorious topic of politics, which is always a hot topic, and certainly does get my blood pressure to rise a little, but not for the reasons you may think. I find the mentality of politics, in most cases, is childlike and immature. I have not seen behaviors like I witness these days since I was in grade school. The mentality that many people have been displaying about political topics is like that of children, not HLTs. The separate points of view are healthy. The manner in which we secure and protect them are not. A HLT does not have all the answers, and does not always know who is right for the leadership position. Their special mental gift is the fact that they are smart enough to know what they don't know.

This chapter is not about my opinion or the opinion of others on political issues. It is about each person's own mentality in seeking the truth and searching for the best solution to serve mankind. It is also the mental process we use to choose those to make the decisions for us. It does not matter if you are a political leader or just a person with an opinion. The truth should always be the goal, along with the realization that your opinion may not be the truth.

If I were to tell one hundred people that their opinion may not be the truth, ninety-nine would be offended and strike back at me. That is because we believe that our own opinion, whether derived from our own facts or from another source is the truth. That is the way our common brain works. It takes a much stronger person—a HLT—to travel to that higher view and seek the truth, even though it may not agree with their opinion and the opinion of their peers.

Now I am going to make a very bold and controversial statement, and I will welcome all challengers on the subject. When you choose sides, whether choosing sides of an opinion or choosing sides for a representative, you quit seeking the truth. Bold talk, right? In my opinion, that is the truth. If you commit yourself to a side, you will mentally quit looking for the truth. It is human nature. Sometimes, it is good to set on the fence for awhile. That way you can see both sides, and not just the side where the grass is greener, because that is just a surface issue. It is better to reserve opinion long enough to find out how strong the root system is, because that is what sustains the grass above. Have you ever heard someone say, "Yes, I voted for Mr. X, but I was wrong," or "I believed my solution was correct, but lately I have been rethinking my position." You haven't, have you? You must go to that higher place and drop your pride. Pride is mixed up in your opinion. Realize that the truth may be that, just because you voted for someone, it doesn't mean they have all the answers. Just because you have a party affiliation, it doesn't mean your party has all the solutions. It is impossible for one man to have all the right answers. If you understand this, you have just broken the code and received a pass to the land of the HLT. In the political arena, we choose to put our faith in one person or one party. Once we have done this, we decide the person we voted for is always right, and the person we voted against is wrong. It has to be, or else it would go against the almighty me.

As a HLT, how can you possibly believe this is true? It is reverse awareness. You will seek out negative information against the opposing person and will only focus on the good traits of your person. The strength of a HLT is the ability to rise above all closed and narrow minds, and open their minds to other opinions. They use all the tools to seek the truth of common sense. In some cases, they admit that they were wrong and continue the fight in finding the path to that truth. Each individual has to search their own mind and soul for that truth. It will be a difficult task since, we as humans, seek out those who believe what we believe. When we find comfort in others that have the same views as we do, we have a tendency to behave like sharks gathering for the feast, and the feast is anyone else with an opposing view or opinion. When you vote for a person, do you honestly believe that he or she actually has all the right answers in this complicated society? If you truly believe that, then you are a LLT, because you have put your beliefs in the impossible. Unfortunately, most of the people you meet believe this. Just because you voted for them, selfish pride will not let you change your mind. Are you understanding this or just reading this? If you come to your senses and admit that your representative does not have all the answers, shouldn't that by theory cause you to open up your mind to other options and opinions? Until we quit choosing sides like it was a game of dodge ball on the playground, will we not be able to move on and solve the important issues with the right people.

Personally speaking, I would estimate that ninety-five percent of the people I discuss any issue with do not know the basic facts of the topic we are discussing—me included. If you do not believe me, next time you are in a interesting discussion about any topic, ask the person you are debating with to give you facts and to prove it—not with another person's words, but with the facts. They will begin the dance, because all they have is their opinion which was created by them or the opinion of someone else with very little facts. So what does this tell you? It tells me that this fake truth was generated from assumptions, not reality. Unfortunately, the feeding frenzy begins and the damage is done. The truth is clouded up by lies and agendas, and the persecution begins.

As we enter the real world of politics, examine yourself and see if I hit a few nerves. Hopefully, I will bring out your new self-empowerment to seek the truth and not give into your peers and the circling sharks.

Entering the Real World

This first example is unfortunately quite common in the political world. This lack of focus goes against one of the trademarks of a HLT. Three people are setting at a table: a Republican, a Democrat, and a HLT. The HLT brings up an issue to be discussed, because this person is eager to solve it. Automatically, the Republican blames the Democratic Party. The Democrat blames the Republican Party, and soon the discussion becomes a blaming game. Instead, it should be a problem-solving mission of individual minds. It becomes very clear that both individuals—the Republican and the Democrat—completely forgot the issue. Sound familiar? The HLT wanted nothing but to seek out both opinions of "the issue" and look for common ground. Unfortunately, it was not going to happen. Their focus was not on the issue, but on the other party. It became the blame game instead of problem solving.

As a Republican or a Democrat, you must still reach down and determine the solution to the problem, no matter how the problem was created or from where the solution might come. A HLT must build their internal strength and security. This is only done by seeking the truth, not by blaming others. This blame game happens every day, all over America, and it happens to me several times a week. What a shame.

The second example is not about the lack of focus or an issue, as in the first example, but one which involves the lack of respect. This also is a true story that once happened to me and it has opened my eyes to the sad reality of the mentality that has developed in our world today.

While overhearing a conversation between two people, I was accidently ushered into the conversation by a comment directed to me. Reluctantly, I entered into this conversation. However, I decided not to approach this issue with my opinion first, but to analyze the respect factor for all participants involved. I opened up my portion of the conversation with one of respect to their opinion and blended my ideas and thoughts with theirs so we could have a higher level conversation about two political candidates. I said I respected anyone who takes on the challenges of a political office. I respect their efforts to make things better and their years of dedication to get to that level so they can make those changes. At first I was talking about the person they were ridiculing and then my appreciation and respect was going to be directed to the person that they were supporting. Before I could get to their representative, I was rudely interrupted and was shamed for suggesting that I respected their opponent. Respect is a tool that is paramount for self growth. I mentioned earlier that respect of one's effort came first, before disagreement. The atmosphere for success must start with respect. This conversation was doomed from the beginning because by first disrespecting the effort of others, they failed to look into the mirror and realize that the person they opposed at least attempted to make things better. Something they had failed to do.

The second point I wanted to make was that they had disrespected me, by not hearing me out. They had not allowed me to give my opinion, whether or not it would have been absorbed in their closed mind or not. What they did not realize is that by this childish mentality they have taken away any credibility of their words and thoughts. Intelligence is born from listening, not talking. By their behavior and their disrespect to me, I could not listen to their opinion that I was so thirsty for, so I could learn. Communication, understanding and learning died in this non-exchange of thoughts and they were never regained.

Respecting a person's efforts and opinions is vital if we are going to become one again in our society. I am afraid it may be too late, and it is our fault.

The third example is a glorious tale of a possible reality. I have seen it, I have felt it, and I have experienced it. It does exist, but unfortunately it is extremely rare. Two men were in a conversation about two candidates running for the same office, both from different parties. In fact, the two men have represented two different parties in the past. The exciting atmosphere on this day was that both men where HLTs and they were both seeking the same goal, the right person for the job. The only difference between two LLTs discussing a topic and two HLTs doing the same is that the LLTs have already made up their minds before they started the discussion, not after they were done.

Every conversation should be one of a new experience and an open mind, not one of you forcing your opinion on others. Listen, learn, and grow together.

Let me get back to my example of these two politically opposite men. The one thing they had abundantly present in their discussion was respect. I have brought up this word before and will again because it is one of the only tools that can break the me-mentality which is the reason walls are built in the first place. These two men were HLTs. They know that their opinions may not be the truth. They know that if they are to learn, they must respect different opinions of an issue or different sides to a candidate that they themselves have failed to explore. They thirst for more knowledge, because that makes them better. Their views may or may not change after they listen to the other view. However, they can now proceed with a better feeling that they have made the right choice because of getting the opposing view. They also can respect themselves, because they were seeking their own truth and did it in a civilized manner, one that was created with an open mind, and one that was built with respect, a mutual respect.

I was one of the men, and for a brief moment in time, I visited the land of the HLT. I know I did, and it felt good. I only wish others could experience the same wonderful feeling. Each opinion was given as a question to the other and it became a learning experience for him and for me. It appeared magical, but it was reality, because it happened. It appeared magical, because it was rare. No one was forcing an opinion on us. We were both seeking more knowledge to find the truth. Now, I cannot tell you who my friend voted for. I cannot tell you that his opinion changed because of my opinion, but I can tell you that my eyes were opened wider than they were before, because I listened to his opinion. Because of that discussion, I see both sides more clearly, including my own. The beauty of that experience and this HLT relationship was that we allowed each other respectfully to go our own way. We entered the voting booth with our own conscience and our own questions answered and without peer pressure or without the media brainwashing. I felt absolutely at peace with my decision. Now, that does not mean that I was right about my decision. I will still hold that feeling that I could be wrong, and I will continue to look for the truth, even when it may be against my beliefs.

The Challenge

I challenge you to accept the fact that you may not know the truth, but continue to seek it. If you were wrong, admit it and continue the fight to find the truth. I challenge you to give your opinion and educate others, because the truth may be your words, but also drink from the mind of others. Broaden your perspective of another side. Normal thinking is accepting what others say. They want you to believe it, because they want validation of their opinion. It is your job as a HLT and my challenge to you to grow that self-empowerment. Seek your own truth. Seek the truth in every person and every situation that arises, without getting clouded by personal influence. The political challenge is in you. Challenge yourself to not be brainwashed by the media, which we all know has its own agendas. Do not be influenced by your own family and friends, because it is quite possible they may not be seeking the truth. I challenge you to believe in your own strength and feel the inner power you have to see the whole picture, not just the picture a particular party or a person paints. I challenge you to feel your mental wisdom grow by dropping your own pride long enough to ask the questions that will find the truth.

The Higher Level View

The truth is what it is. It may not be discovered until all the smoke clears. Sooner or later the truth will emerge, so keep that in mind. Most people involved in an issue will not know if your opinion was correct until the future has a chance to reveal the past. Be cautious when pushing your opinion too hard. It may backfire when "the truth" comes out. Politics is mostly based on opinions and emotions, not facts. This chapter is about destroying the me-society, which I do believe is like a runaway train and may not be able to slow down or stop. However, that is what it will take to become a society of unity once again. We will have a different opinion about issues and who we like as candidates. Actually, that is a good and a healthy thing. It is the stubborn mentality within us that makes matters worse. This includes the politician who makes the decisions and the people who put them there.

HLTs do not make things difficult. They focus on the issue at hand, open up all avenues of thought, and proceed with only one goal in mind: to seek the truth no matter where it comes from. I am fortunate to have experienced a HLT conversation and have not been in one since. I continue to look for it, though. How sad is that? Everyone has their own opinion. Unfortunately, it is already secured in mental concrete, and that is a shame. To be open to new ideas and able to show respect is a great feeling, and it will be rewarded by a great feeling of pride.

So now if you want to talk politics with me, welcome my fellow HLTs. Bring your ideas, both negative and positive. Bring your voice of solutions. Bring your ears, so you can hear mine, and bring your respect and your passion for unity, so we can solve our differences and seek the truth.

The HLT Voter

The HLT voter seeks the truth and will even disregard their short-term opinion by realizing the long-term effects of the opposite opinion may be better. They will seek character over words and will be careful to search all avenues for their answers. They will not be influenced by family, friends and the media. They will search their soul for common sense, knowing it will trump any political party affiliation. They know that their self-empowerment is created by the fact that they will vote their own conscience. With their self-empowerment, they will now choose a person that possesses the characteristics that a HLT represents.

The HLT Political Leader

The HLT leader, President, Congressman and Governor must all play the party game to get elected. That is the law of the land, and it will not change. So first, they must side with a "party" or they will not get elected. They must have the sly intelligence to get into the position to make changes. This is where the HLT comes out. After being elected, they must turn to the people and say, "I am no longer affiliated with a party. I am no longer a Republican or a Democrat. I am your servant. I am a gatherer of minds to solve the issues that confront us, all of us. I am the representative of all people and the deliverer of common sense." Then, as a HLT, you will walk the walk as an independent spirit searching for the truth. Their reward will be that self-empowered peace that only honesty and integrity can bring.

HLT Summary

To my wonderful brothers and sisters on this earth, I have tried in so many ways to open your mind up to the power of a higher level of thinking. My intentions in this book were not to degrade anyone or to give the impression that anyone is better than anyone else. It is to remind everyone who reads this book that they have this incredible gift from our Creator called the mind. If used properly, it can bring more peace into your life and less troubled waters.

I am sure at times this book has made you mad and probably a little defensive. That was all by design, because it made you think. So, if you were either questioning my thoughts or absorbing my words, I was successful. This book was not intended for me to tell you which mental level you live in. It was designed so you would care enough about your own life and the lives of those around you to self-examine your own mental awareness. By that mental awareness, I hope you will decide to challenge your own weaknesses and do something about them. Take charge of your life and make a positive impact on life situations, instead of letting life happen to you.

There are exceptions to every rule or thought that I have written about. However, exceptions are just a small step away from excuses, and a HLT does not believe in those. A HLT believes that almost every situation in life becomes their responsibility to one degree or another. It is either in the way they take charge of it or the way they handle it.

Not once did I say I was perfect, and not once did I say I have not made mistakes. I will, however, make the statement that every mistake was met with a lesson learned and a mentality which has groomed me to teach. Maybe I am asking for the impossible, but it is only because I care too much about people to see pain. So, I will take this chance to be defeated in the quest for being victorious to change lives.

I wrote this book because I do care, and I am tired of people suffering. I am tired of hearing about the bad relationships that could have been avoided if communication was part of their life. I am tired of the financial ruin caused by people's inner ego winning the battle and taking over their common sense. I am devastated every time I hear of a vehicle accident that could have been avoided. The greedy seconds of time that someone tried to save that took a precious life from this earth. I would gladly trade years of my life just to have them back.

Bad relationships, financial problems, and accidents do not just happen. The trickle down of bad happenings begins with the seed of bad thoughts or no thoughts at all. The one thing that I have learned about life is that your actions, good or bad, will affect others, and those of others will affect you. You need to make sure that the bad events are not created by your own lack of thought or your lack of action or your bad actions. Because of my real life examples, I hope you are now more aware of your weaknesses and can now be the solution instead of the problem. I am not a writer. I am just a man with a message that stands for goodness, giving, and prosperity. I know I have been given a gift to know the difference and to make a difference with that knowledge. I have made mistakes in my past and will make mistakes in my future. However, because of my awareness of those mistakes made by me, and my awareness of the mistakes made by others, my life should be more peaceful, more productive, and more giving.

By my observation, the people in our world are becoming more reckless, more judgmental, more disrespectful, and selfish as every day goes by. The fact is it can begin to turn the other way if you yourself live up to a standard of class and intelligence, and by seeking the unselfish truth.

As your self-empowerment becomes strong, you can lead by example and begin teaching common sense intelligence that will spread like the giant rocks in the foundation of the pyramids of Egypt. Through this, new worlds are built, and giving can grow, and safety will flourish, and tragedies will be avoided.

Your God has given you the most wonderful gifts. The heart is a great one, but the mind has to listen and act on what the heart is telling it. This is fact, and I live my life by these words: I will try every day to do my job. I will try everyday to not cause pain on others, and I will try every day to make this world a better place by being unselfish and giving to others, so they can also have a great life.

I know I can change a life every day. Maybe it is just a smile and friendly hello to brighten a person's day. Maybe it is paying for a toll on the freeway for someone behind me. Maybe it is helping someone financially without wanting paid back. Maybe it is focusing on my driving and letting caution rule to insure safety for all. Maybe it is solving my issues myself and making good choices so that it doesn't put the burden either emotionally or financially on someone else.

Being a HLT brings peace and prosperity to your life. I believe it does come from above and, hopefully, enters and is absorbed within. It becomes part of you and every day and every action will be about doing the right things and preventing the wrong things from occurring. Being a HLT is not about intelligence. It is about the personal responsibility of a human being to be safe and content, and to attempt to make everyone else around you safe and content.

As I finished this book a friend of mine went bankrupt. I read in the paper where a young lady passed a car in the fog and hit an oncoming car and lost her life. I found out a couple I knew were getting a divorce. Life is real, and we all better wake up.

I have a cousin who is like a sister to me. She always asks me if I have had any deep thoughts lately. I will leave you with this one, which I believe sums up a HLT. How great would life be if all of us would walk through life not just praising our Lord as a third party, but absorbing his unselfish mind with ours? By this action, we assume the responsibility of looking through our eyes as if they were his eyes. Everything we see, he sees. It is as if we see as one. We see for him, and through him we help fix what is wrong, and with his mind as ours, we prevent what has not happened yet.

"The most honorable gift we can give is to use the gift we have received from the giver, and that giver is GOD, and his gift is the mind." Douglas K. Reiser

CPSIA information can be obtained at www.ICGtesting.com
Printed in the USA
LVOW05s2015040114

368094LV00021B/1318/P